CAMPAIGN • 144

WAKE ISLAND 1941

A battle to make the gods weep

JIM MORAN

ILLUSTRATED BY PETER DENNIS

Series editor Marcus Cowper

First published in 2011 by Osprey Publishing
Midland House, West Way, Botley, Oxford OX2 0PH, UK
44-02 23rd St, Suite 219, Long Island City, NY 11101, USA

E-mail: info@ospreypublishing.com

Print ISBN: 978 1 84908 603 5
PDF e-book ISBN: 978 1 84908 604 2
EPUB e-book ISBN: 978 1 84908 943 2

Editorial by Ilios Publishing Ltd, Oxford, UK (www.iliospublishing.com)
Design: The Black Spot
Index by Marie-Pierre Evans
Originated by Blenheim Colour Ltd
Maps by Bounford.com
Bird's-eye view artworks: The Black Spot
Printed in China through World Print Ltd.

11 12 13 14 15 10 9 8 7 6 5 4 3 2 1

www.ospreypublishing.com

ACKNOWLEDGMENTS

Special thanks are given to the United States Marine Corps Research Center, MCCDC Quantico, Virginia – in particular to Mike Miller and John Lyles, without whose invaluable help this book would not have been possible. Thanks are also given to Major Richard T. Spooner and Colonel Elliot Laine, Jr., USMC Ret., for their assistance in the research for this project.

AUTHOR'S NOTE

Wake Island, 19° 18'N, 166° 37'E, lies west of the International Date Line and so is one day ahead of the mainland United States. All dates and times in this narrative will be local to Wake. Wake Island is in fact an atoll made up of three islands within a reef-enclosed lagoon: Wake Island (Wake proper), Wilkes Island, and Peale Island, but in order to prevent confusion "Wake" will refer to the whole atoll and "Wake proper" will refer to Wake Island itself throughout this book.

ARTIST'S NOTE

Readers may care to note that the original paintings from which the color plates in this book were prepared are available for private sale. The Publishers retain all reproduction copyright whatsoever. All enquiries should be addressed to:

Peter Dennis, Fieldhead, The Park, Mansfield, Notts, NG18 2AT

Email: magie.h@ntlworld.com

The Publishers regret that they can enter into no correspondence upon this matter.

THE WOODLAND TRUST

Osprey Publishing are supporting the Woodland Trust, the UK's leading woodland conservation charity, by funding the dedication of trees.

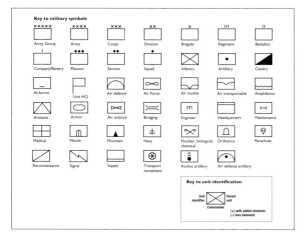

CONTENTS

Situation in the Pacific, December 1941

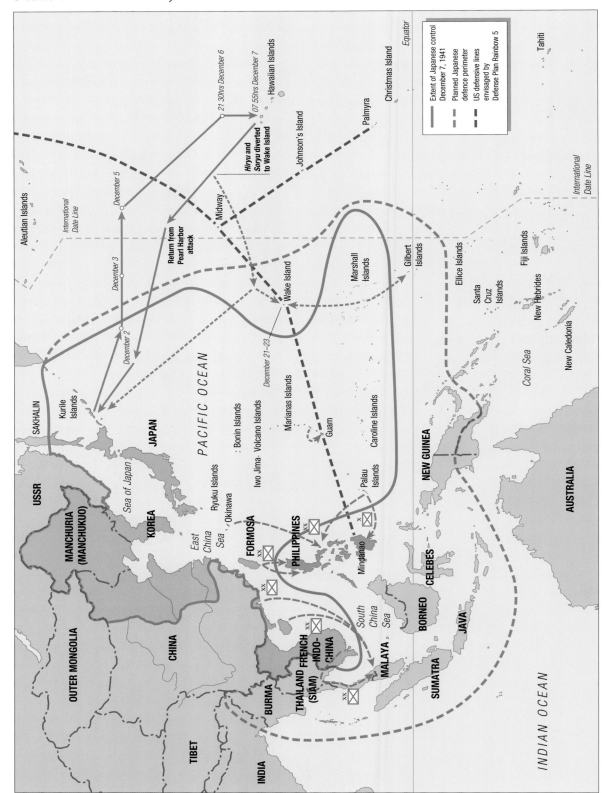

Equator

Aleutian Islands

International Date Line

SAKHALIN

Kurile Islands

JAPAN

USSR

MANCHURIA (MANCHUKUO)

OUTER MONGOLIA

KOREA

Sea of Japan

Ryuku Islands

Okinawa

East China Sea

CHINA

TIBET

INDIA

BURMA

THAILAND (SIAM)

FRENCH INDO-CHINA

MALAYA

SUMATRA

South China Sea

BORNEO

JAVA

CELEBES

NEW GUINEA

AUSTRALIA

PACIFIC OCEAN

Bonin Islands

Iwo Jima · Volcano Islands

Marianas Islands

Guam

Caroline Islands

Palau Islands

Mindanao

PHILIPPINES

FORMOSA

Wake Island

December 21–23

Marshall Islands

Gilbert Islands

Ellice Islands

Santa Cruz Islands

New Hebrides

Fiji Islands

New Caledonia

Coral Sea

INDIAN OCEAN

Midway

Johnson's Island

Hawaiian Islands

07 55hrs December 7

21 30hrs December 6

December 5

December 3

December 2

Return from Pearl Harbor attack

Hiryu and Soryu diverted to Wake Island

Palmyra

Christmas Island

Tahiti

International Date Line

International Date Line

- Extent of Japanese control December 7, 1941
- Planned Japanese defence perimeter
- US defensive lines envisaged by Defense Plan Rainbow 5

ORIGINS OF THE CAMPAIGN

Morrison Knudson memorial to the CPNAB contractors of Wake Island. (Author's collection)

Covering some 2,600 acres, the atoll of Wake Island is roughly 4.5 miles (7.2km) long by 2.25 miles (3.6km) wide and is "V-" or "wishbone"-shaped, with Wake proper making up the center section of the wishbone to the south and east, with Peale on the northwest prong, and Wilkes the southwest prong. Deep water surrounds the lagoon, inside a barrier reef that itself is 30–1,100yds (27–1,006m) wide with occasional potholes and large boulders.

Three passageways open into the lagoon; one is the open end of the wishbone to the northwest, and the other two openings are the channels between Wake proper and Wilkes and Peale Islands. Peale and Wake proper are connected by two wooden bridges spanning the channel. Only the channel between Wilkes and Wake proper allows access to the lagoon by shallow-draught vessels, and so all cargo has to be landed on Wilkes' southern shore and transferred either by boat across the lagoon to Peale Island or by using the crushed-coral road that runs from Wake proper around to Peale.

All three islands have white coral beaches ranging from 20–170yds (18–155m) wide, sloping gently from the shoreline to the vegetation line. Elevation is a maximum of only 21ft (6.4m), with an average of 12ft (3.6m), and the majority of all three islands are covered by thick, tropical shrubs and grasses, interspersed with trees that reach a height of 20–25ft (6–7.6m) only

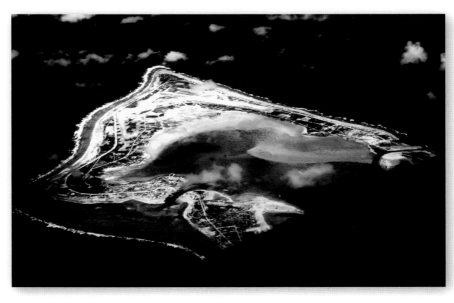

This photograph gives a good overall view of Wake Island, including the reefs that surround it. The only land for hundreds of miles, it was a vital strategic location in 1941. (Getty)

(in 1941 there were no palm trees on the atoll). These shrubs and grasses initially provided excellent cover and camouflage for the defenders and the civilian contractors, but also conferred this advantage to the Japanese forces once they had landed. The islands are made up of disintegrated coral with sparse soil, making drainage very good, but this also precludes the existence of any freshwater supply. Rainfall is light and temperatures range from 68–95 °F (20–25 °C).

Wake Island's strategic importance was recognized long before hostilities commenced between the United States and Japan. In 1796 Captain Wake located the atoll accurately, landed, and named it after himself. In 1840 Charles Wilkes USN landed with a survey party including the naturalist Titian Peale, and stayed for several weeks, sampling and surveying. Wilkes named the southwest island after himself and the northwest island after Titian Peale.

The only major excitement to happen on Wake prior to the arrival of Pan American Airways (PanAm) was on March 5, 1866, when the German bark *Libelle* was wrecked on the reef east of Wake proper. The survivors made it to shore along with an alleged money cargo of $300,000 and, after three weeks, left Wake in two of the ship's boats in an attempt to reach Guam. One boat of mixed passengers and crew, including the famous opera singer Anna Bishop, made it to safety after 18 days at sea. The other boat, with eight people on board, including the *Libelle*'s captain, was never heard from again. Pieces of the *Libelle* were still being found by construction workers in 1940. What became of the $300,000 money cargo remains a mystery.

On January 17, 1899, the USS *Bennington*, commanded by Commander Edward Taussig USN, "took possession of the atoll known as Wake Island for the United States of America." In 1934 jurisdiction over Wake was passed to the US Navy Department and in 1935 permission was granted to PanAm to establish an intermediate base for the trans-Pacific flying-boat "clipper" service to the Far East. The US Navy was quick to realize the potential military value of PanAm's development on Wake, giving the company every assistance in the base's construction. Work started on the base on May 5, 1935, and progressed at such a pace that the first landing by a PanAm clipper into Wake's lagoon was on August 9, 1935.

In May 1938 the US Congress instituted a strategic survey for the needs of additional naval bases and facilities, to be handled by Rear Admiral A. J. Hepburn USN. This was the so-called "Hepburn Board." In his report Hepburn made many recommendations, most of which were incorporated as part of US defense strategy. With regard to Wake, the Board afforded it high priority as a base and recommended a $7,500,000 three-year development program to turn Wake into an airbase for long-range patrol and reconnaissance planes, as well as an intermediate station on the air route to the Far East. In the words of the report: "The immediate continuous operation of patrol planes from Wake would be vital at the outbreak of war in the Pacific."

By April 18, 1941, the Commander-in-Chief, United States Pacific Fleet, Admiral Husband E. Kimmel USN, being fully aware of Wake's strategic significance, was becoming more and more alarmed about Wake's defensive capability in the event of war with Japan. Kimmel expressed his concerns to the Chief of Naval Operations (CNO), highlighting that Wake was:

2,000 miles [3,200km] from Pearl Harbor, over 1,000 miles [1,600km] from Midway and about 1,400 miles [2,250km] from Johnston… On the other hand it is but 450 miles [725km] from Bikini in the Marshalls, while Marcus, which itself is an outpost of the Bonins and Marianas, is 765 miles [1,230km] to the northwestward… As an operating patrol plane base, it could prove highly valuable to us in observing the Marshalls, or in covering advance of our forces toward the Saipan–Honshu line. In the hands of the Japanese, it would be a serious obstacle to surprise raids in the Northern Marshalls, or on Marcus, Port Lloyd [Port Lloyd was the principal port on Chichi Jima in the Bonins. It was then highly regarded by planners as a key point in Western Pacific strategy, although Chichi Jima's sister island would be better remembered in history – Iwo Jima] or Saipan … and would be capable of causing serious interference with other secret movements of our forces…

An illustration of the "globe and anchor" device, the insignia of the United States Marine Corps, displaying its famous motto of "semper fidelis" ("always faithful"). It has in itself become part of the Marines' legend, which was strengthened further by the media portrayal of the battle of Wake Island. (USMC)

Imperial Japanese Navy SNLF troops, the equivalent in the Japanese Navy to the US Marines, here shown manning a Type 92 heavy machine gun. These men would form the core of the assault force on Wake. (Author's collection)

To deny Wake to the enemy, without occupying it ourselves would be difficult; to recapture it if the Japanese should seize it in the early period of hostilities would require operations of some magnitude…

If Wake be defended, then for the Japanese to reduce it would require extended operations of their naval force in an area where we might be able to get at them; thus affording us opportunity to get at naval forces with naval forces… We should try, by every possible means, to get the Japanese to expose naval units. In order to do this, we must provide objectives that require such exposure.

With the foregoing considerations in mind, it is considered essential that the construction work now in progress on Wake be proceeded with and that the eventuality of war should not interrupt it. To this end, the Commander in Chief, Pacific Fleet, believes that defense installations and defense forces should be established on Wake at the earliest possible date, even at the expense of slowing down construction. It may be pointed out, in this connection, that in the absence of defense forces, construction on Wake, in the event of war, is subject to serious interruption or even complete stoppage, through enemy action.

It is therefore recommended that units of a marine defense battalion be progressively established on Wake as facilities there permit.

Kimmel's words did not go unheeded and steps were implemented to dispatch defense capabilities to Wake "as soon as practicable." By the Autumn of 1941 Wake was one huge building site with over 1,200 construction workers from Morrison-Knudson Co, part of the consortium Contractors Pacific Naval Air Bases (CPNAB), which had been formed in 1941 to carry out works on the islands on behalf of the US Navy. In addition to the construction workers working feverishly on the Navy project, US Marine Corps defense personnel from the 1st Defense Battalion and Aircraft Fighting Squadron 211 along with Navy and Army units were busy preparing defense installations throughout the islands when an ominous dispatch was received from Pearl Harbor in November, warning that the "international situation indicates you should be on the alert."

CHRONOLOGY

1941

January 9   United States Navy pioneer party and first contingent of contractors for CPNAB arrive and commence construction of naval-base facilities on Wake, under the command of Lieutenant Commander Elmer Greey USN and CPNAB Superintendent Dan Teters.

August 19   Advance party, 1st Defense Battalion, Fleet Marine Force (FMF), arrives and makes camp (Camp 1) under the command of Major Lewis Hohn.

October 15   Major James Devereux assumes duty as island commander and Marine detachment commander.

November 2   200 Marine reinforcements arrive at Wake on the USS *Castor*.

November 29 VMF-211's advance party, under the command of Major Walter Bayler, arrives and commences preparations to receive aircraft. Commander Winfield Cunningham arrives and relieves Maj. Devereux as island commander.

December 4   VMF-211, under the command of Major Paul Putnam, flies in to Wake from USS *Enterprise*.

December 8   First Japanese air raid on Wake by land-based bombers from the 24th Air Flotilla. Seven fighter planes of VMF-211 are destroyed and there are numerous casualties.

December 9   Second Japanese air raid on Wake.

December 10 Third Japanese air raid on Wake. A dynamite cache, with 125 tons of explosives, is blown up on Wilkes with major damage to batteries on that island.

December 11 The Japanese, under the command of Rear Admiral Sadamichi Kajioka, attempt to land on Wake and are decisively defeated with the loss of two destroyers and with major damage to three cruisers, three destroyers, one destroyer-transport, and one transport. Fourth Japanese air raid on Wake.

December 12	Fifth Japanese air raid on Wake. Japanese submarine bombed and possibly sunk by VMF-211 25 miles (40km) southwest of Wake. Mass burial services are held after nightfall.
December 14	Sixth and seventh Japanese air raids on Wake.
December 15	Eighth Japanese air raid on Wake.
December 15–16	Relief force (Task Force 14) sets sail from Pearl Harbor.
December 16	Ninth and tenth Japanese air raids on Wake.
December 17	11th and 12th Japanese air raids on Wake.
December 18	Japanese photoreconnaissance conducted over Wake. Task Group 7.2, composed of SS *Triton* and SS *Tambor*, is withdrawn from Wake.
December 19	13th Japanese air raid on Wake.
December 20	A PBY seaplane arrives from Midway with information about the relief expedition.
December 21	The PBY departs from Wake with the last United States personnel to leave the atoll. 14th Japanese air raid on Wake (first large carrier strike by planes from carriers *Hiryu* and *Soryu*), followed by 15th Japanese air raid on Wake.
December 22	16th Japanese air raid on Wake. The last two aircraft of VMF-211 are rendered inoperable and the squadron reports to defense-detachment commander as infantry. Task Force 14 stops to refuel, 515 miles (830km) from Wake.

The Marines defending Wake Island were all specialists, but in the Marine Corps first and foremost every Marine is a rifleman.

December 23	2nd Maizuru Second Special Naval Landing Force (SNLF) executes pre-dawn landing on southern shore of Wake proper and Wilkes and, after almost 12 hours' fighting, the defenders of Wake Island surrender. Task Force 14 is recalled.

1942

January 12	United States prisoners of war are evacuated from Wake for confinement in the Japanese Empire.
February 24	First United States carrier strikes on Wake.

1943

July 8	Eight Army B-24s make first land-based strike against Wake, operating from Midway. Succeeding shore-based air raids continue at intervals.
October 6–7	Major US carrier strikes on Wake.
October 7	The 98 US civilian prisoners remaining on Wake are executed on the order of Rear Admiral Sakaibara.

1944

January–May	996 US sorties are delivered against Wake, dropping 1,079 tons of bombs. Naval bombardment fires 7,092 shells at the islands.
September–October	Repeated strikes on Wake by Army B-24s.

1945

January–June	Repeated sorties by US Navy shore-based PBY squadrons.
July	Major naval bombardment of Wake.
August 13	Last United States air raid on Wake (executed by Marine Corps aircraft against Peacock Point battery).
September 7	Rear Admiral Sakaibara surrenders Wake to Brigadier-General Lawson Sanderson.

1947

June 18	Rear Admiral Sakaibara is hanged for the massacre of 98 civilian construction workers on Wake.

OPPOSING COMMANDERS

US COMMANDERS

As part of the overall US defense strategy in place at the time (the latest version being codenamed *Rainbow 5*), Wake came under the jurisdiction of the 14th Naval District Commandant, **Admiral Kimmel**, with headquarters at Pearl Harbor, even though Wake was some 2,000 miles (3,200km) from Pearl Harbor.

Kimmel was a very competent commander. Born on February 26, 1882, in Henderson, Kentucky, he was married with two sons and had graduated from the US Naval Academy in 1904. Prior to his promotion to rear admiral in 1937 Kimmel had served on several battleships, commanded two destroyer divisions, and commanded the USS *New York*. In 1939 he was appointed to the post of Commander of Cruisers Battle Force.

In February of 1941, Kimmel replaced Admiral James Richardson as Commander-in-Chief, US Fleet and Pacific Fleet, with the temporary rank of full admiral. In May 1940 the Pacific Fleet had moved its headquarters from its traditional home of San Diego, California, to its new home at Pearl Harbor, and shortly after taking command in February 1941 Kimmel expressed his deep concerns to the CNO over this location, pointing out its vulnerability to "surprise attack by submarine, air or combined forces." These words would prove to be prescient.

The USS *William Ward Burrows*. In January of 1941 the *Burrows* transported the first load of construction equipment and personnel from Hawaii to Wake. In October 1941 it delivered the 1st Defense Battalion's commanding officer, Maj. Devereux. (NARA)

Kimmel was fully aware of the strategic value of Wake and he made every effort to turn the atoll into the stronghold it was intended to be. Thus, in June 1941 elements of the 1st Defense Battalion were directed to establish defenses at Wake. With the attack on Pearl Harbor on December 7, 1941, Kimmel instigated plans for a relief force to reinforce Wake's defenses and possibly lure the Japanese Navy into a pitched sea battle, partly to avenge Pearl Harbor, but in mid-December Kimmel was relieved of his command and his plans would come to nothing. Admiral Kimmel retired early in 1942 and spent much of his retirement defending his involvement in the Pearl Harbor debacle. He died on May 14, 1968.

Admiral Kimmel was relieved by **Vice Admiral William Pye**, who held the temporary post until the arrival of Admiral Chester Nimitz, who took over the command on December 31, 1941. Pye was born in Minneapolis, Minnesota, on June 9, 1880; he graduated from the US Naval Academy in 1901 and prior to World War II served on several ships, being commended for excellent performance of his duties as part of the Atlantic Fleet during World War I. During the 1920s and 1930s Pye commanded the USS *Oglala* (CM-4) and the USS *Nevada* (BB-36) and, following promotion to rear admiral, Pye became chief of staff of the Scouting Force, and attended the Naval War College. With the temporary rank of vice admiral, Pye was Commander Battle Force in 1941 at Pearl Harbor, with his flag on the USS *California*. Pye was on the *California* when the Japanese attacked on December 7.

Commander Winfield Scott Cunningham took over as island commander from Maj. Devereux. Cunningham would leave the defense of Wake to Devereux, but it would be Cunningham who made the final decision to surrender. (USMC)

Considered to be still shaken from the December 7 attack following his appointment as Kimmel's replacement, Pye had little enthusiasm for Kimmel's plans for a relief force to Wake. Although he did authorize its departure, he would ultimately recall the force on December 23, an action for which many would never forgive him.

After handing over command to Admiral Nimitz on December 31, 1941, Pye became commander of Task Force One, based in San Francisco, patrolling the West Coast out to Hawaii, but was relieved in October 1942. Pye would never command operating forces again and he retired in July 1944.

Officer in Charge, Naval Activities, Wake Island and island commander was **Commander Winfield Scott Cunningham USN**. Born on February 16, 1900, in Rockbridge, Wisconsin, Cunningham entered the United States Naval Academy in 1916, graduating in June of 1919. As an ensign he served on the USS *Martha* in the Mediterranean off the coast of Turkey. In 1922 he sailed for China aboard the USS *Huron*, where he spent the next two and a half years, returning to the US as a lieutenant (junior grade) in May 1923. Whilst serving in China, Cunningham first applied for aviation training but was turned down. However, finally, after several attempts, he was accepted in 1924. He reported to the Naval Air Station, Pensacola, Florida, as a student naval aviator in February 1925. Cunningham was promoted to lieutenant in June 1925 and was designated a naval aviator in September 1925. He served aboard the aircraft carrier USS *Langley*, serving at the Naval Air Station, Pearl Harbor, for two years. In 1935 Cunningham reported as executive officer of Fighting Plane Squadron 2 aboard the USS *Lexington*, and one year later took command of Fighting Plane Squadron 5 aboard the USS *Yorktown*.

From 1938 to 1940 Cunningham ran the Naval Reserve Aviation Base at Oakland, California, before becoming navigator of the USS *Wright*. Whilst serving aboard the *Wright*, Cunningham received orders detaching him for

In what became a famous recruiting poster for the USMC, this man poses with an M1903 Springfield rifle. This was the standard rifle used by the USMC at the time of the battle of Wake Island. (United States National Archives)

service at Naval Air Station, Wake Island. Reporting to Admiral Bloch at Pearl Harbor, Cunningham received little assistance in respect of his new role of island commander, only being told by Bloch's chief of staff, Captain Earle, of the paramount importance of the works being carried out by the CPNAB contractors already on Wake; at no time was Cunningham told of the possibility of Wake being an early target for the Japanese in the event of war.

On November 28, 1941, Cunningham stepped ashore on Wake and assumed the duties of "Officer in Charge of Naval Activities, Wake Island," taking over from Maj. Devereux with a simple exchange of salutes. Cunningham was a very different man from Maj. Devereux; he worked quietly with his subordinates, rarely raising his voice, and preferred to let his officers get on with their jobs with as little interference as possible. Considered by many to be a "perfect gentleman," Cunningham could also be very stubborn, and once he had made a decision it would be almost impossible to get him to change his mind; this would be demonstrated many times during the siege of Wake.

Although a very competent aviator, Cunningham had little experience with coastal defense and as such left the defense works in the capable hands of Maj. Devereux. Cunningham spent most of his time initially with the CPNAB superintendent Dan Teters and at the temporary naval office he established at Camp 2 (the CPNAB contractors' camp). By the time of his arrival, Cunningham found the majority of construction work well under way, with work on all the major installations in progress, including the airstrip. He looked forward to the arrival of the VMF-211 aviation unit, whose ground crews arrived with him on November 28.

After the arrival of the 12 Wildcats of VMF-211, Cunningham spent a lot of time with the unit's commander, Maj. Putnam, formulating defense plans to the point of almost ignoring the presence of Maj. Devereux and his defense battalion; this would lead to problems of command during the siege and fan the flames of the "Cunningham–Devereux controversy" after the fall of Wake, a dispute that would last right up to Cunningham's death in 1986. Cunningham remained in contact with Pearl Harbor throughout the siege and it was he who made the final decision to surrender the island.

Temporary island commander until the arrival of Cdr. Cunningham, and commanding officer of 1st Defense Battalion, was **Major James Devereux**. Devereux was born on February 20, 1903, in Cabana, Cuba, where his army-surgeon father was stationed. The Devereux family moved to Chevy Chase, Maryland, in 1910, where James, one of ten children, attended Army and Navy Preparatory School in Washington, DC, becoming amongst other things a most accomplished horseman. Whilst the family was stationed in Vienna, Austria, James attended La Villa school in Lausanne, Switzerland. Upon their return to the United States James attended Loyola College, Baltimore,

Maryland. Devereux was very proud of his heritage and claimed that his family history could be traced back to Robert Devereux, Earl of Essex, the reputed lover of Queen Elizabeth I of England, and even back to the Norman Conquest in 1066.

Devereux served as both an enlisted man and officer in the United States Marine Corps; he enlisted in July 1923 and in February of 1925 was commissioned as a 2nd lieutenant. Far from the iconic image of a Marine Corps officer, Maj. Devereux at 37 years old was a short (5ft 2in.) and wiry man with a receding hairline and pronounced ears. On October 15, 1941, Devereux arrived on Wake Island and took command of the 1st Defense Battalion. Also, by virtue of seniority, Devereux became island commander, a post he held until the arrival of Cdr. Cunningham. Devereux found plenty to do to render Wake ready for war and instituted a back-breaking program upon his Marines; this would only enhance his reputation as a "by-the-book" officer to his men, who had already crowned him the most hated man in the 1st Defense Battalion.

The only air support Wake had during the 16-day siege came from the 12 F4F-3 Wildcats of VMF-211, commanded by **Major Paul Putnam**. Putnam was a complete contrast to Maj. Devereux; whilst calm and quiet, Putnam never asked anything of his men which he would not do himself. Brave and courageous, he was liked by all.

JAPANESE COMMANDERS

The capture of Wake Island was part of the Japanese war strategy, and fell under the jurisdiction of the IJN Fourth Fleet under the command of **Admiral Shigeyoshi Inoue**. Born on December 9, 1889, in Sendai in the Tohoku region of Japan, Inoue attended the Imperial Japanese Naval Academy, graduating in 1909. As a midshipman, Inoue served on several ships, including the *Soya* on its cruise to Manila, Brisbane, Sydney, Melbourne, Singapore, Hong Kong, and Keelung.

In December 1910 Inoue was promoted to ensign and assigned to the cruiser *Kurama*, where he attended ceremonies for King George V in London in 1911. In 1912 Inoue attended Naval College, studying naval artillery and submarine warfare and was promoted to sub lieutenant in the same year.

SNLF soldiers wade ashore at Balabac Island. They show how the men of 2nd Maizuru SNLF would have been equipped for their amphibious assault on Wake Island. Note the commanding officer standing with arms folded in the middle of the boat. (Mainichi Press)

Major Devereux's command bunker. It is one of the remaining three bunkers on Wake that have stood the test of time and the ravages of Pacific typhoons. (Author's collection)

During World War I, Inoue served on board the battleship *Fuso*, and although the *Fuso* participated in operations against the Imperial German Navy, Inoue saw no actual combat. After the end of World War I, Inoue served as military attaché to Switzerland, learning German and French, and he was part of the Japanese diplomatic delegation to the Paris Peace Talks. In December 1921, Inoue was promoted to lieutenant commander and returned to Japan.

After attending Naval Staff College, Inoue was promoted to commander, holding several staff commissions including that of Naval Attaché to Italy from 1927–29, when he was promoted to captain.

After a brief time at sea as captain of the battleship *Hiei* in 1933, Inoue returned to dry land in November 1935 after his promotion to rear admiral with the position of vice commander of the IJN's 3rd Fleet. Further promoted in 1939 to vice admiral, Inoue took the post of commander of the IJN Aviation Bureau in 1940, where he submitted a radical restructuring of the IJN, advocating the use of air power rather than sea power and the building of aircraft carriers over battleships. This did not go down well at all with IJN high command, and as a result Inoue was given command of the backwater 4th Fleet in 1941, with his headquarters at Truk. Admiral Inoue's flag flew on the light cruiser *Kashima*.

Inoue was a great believer in air power, coming from the same school of ideas as Admiral Yamamoto, and saw only too well the advantages of Wake being part of the Japanese defense perimeter. So, upon receiving orders to take

Wake in the event of war, he formulated the plans for its reduction and capture. It is ironic that for such an advocate of air power and the aircraft carrier, Inoue had no carriers or indeed battleships in his 4th Fleet command.

The task of capturing Wake was given by Admiral Inoue to **Rear Admiral Sadamichi Kajioka**. Kajioka was born in Ehime prefecture, Japan, on May 18, 1891. He graduated from the Imperial Japanese Naval Academy in 1911 and served as midshipman aboard the cruisers *Aso* and *Tokiwa* before being promoted to ensign aboard the cruiser *Akitsushima*. Trained in navigation, Kajioka was promoted to lieutenant and served as chief navigator, first aboard the cruiser *Kiso*, and later the cruisers *Chikuma* and *Kasuga*.

Promoted to lieutenant commander in 1924, Kajioka served aboard the cruisers *Asama* and *Nachi* and the battleship *Mutsu* as chief navigator.

In December 1935 he was promoted to captain and given his first command of a warship as captain of the cruiser *Nagara*; he subsequently went on to command the cruisers *Kasuga* and *Kiso*. Kajioka was promoted to the rank of rear admiral in November of 1940 and given command of Destroyer Squadron 6, with his flag on the light cruiser *Yubari*, part of Admiral Inoue's 4th Fleet. Kajioka was given the command of Wake Island Invasion Force by Admiral Inoue in November 1941.

Totally underestimating Wake's defensive capabilities, and misled by reports from the aerial-bombardment squadrons tasked with "softening up" Wake – they reported all aircraft and major defense emplacements destroyed – Kajioka's first invasion attempt failed dramatically on December 11, the invasion fleet limping back to base with two ships lost and several damaged.

Unusual for the Japanese High Command, Kajioka was not relieved of his command. Instead, he received much more assistance from Admiral Inoue in the way of ships and men, and this time carrier air support for his second attempt at capturing Wake; this attempt would be successful.

After the fall of Wake it is likely that the surviving defenders avoided being executed only by the personal intervention of Rear Admiral Kajioka.

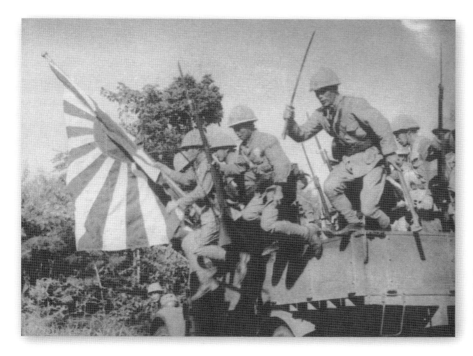

One of these SNLF troops carries a large "Rising Sun" flag, as the men who attacked Wake Island did. Note also the man wielding a traditional Japanese katana sword. (Mainichi Press)

OPPOSING FORCES

US FORCES ON WAKE

On June 23, 1941, Admiral Kimmel received permission to "Progressively establish the appropriate Marine units on Wake as soon as facilities there permit." The Navy originally intended that 4th Defense Battalion was to be Wake's defensive garrison, but it was still at Guantanamo in Cuba, and so, rather than wait any longer, orders were issued to the 1st Defense Battalion, which already had units on Hawaii as well as Johnston and Palmyra Islands.

On August 8, 1941, the USS *Regulus* sortied out of Pearl Harbor; on board were five officers and 170 enlisted men of 1st Defense Battalion under the temporary command of Major Lewis Hohn of the 6th Defense Battalion, as the 1st Battalion had no available field officer spare at that time.

A 3in. gun set up for antiair defense. It was these guns that provided the mainstay of Wake's antiair defense, and successfully damaged several Japanese bombers. (USMC)

Wake Island defensive positions

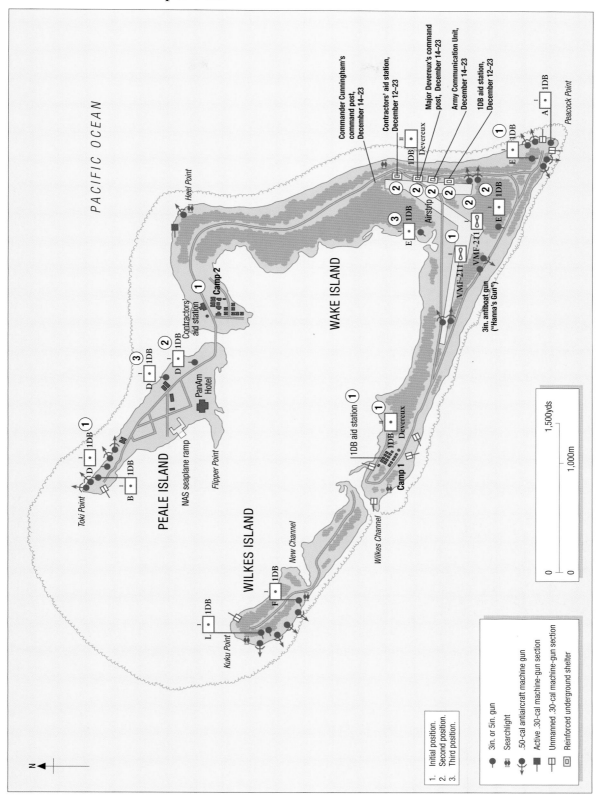

PACIFIC OCEAN

Heel Point

Toki Point

PEALE ISLAND

Flipper Point

Kuku Point

WILKES ISLAND

New Channel

Wilkes Channel

WAKE ISLAND

Peacock Point

Camp 1

Camp 2

PanAm Hotel

NAS seaplane ramp

Contractors' aid station

1DB aid station

Devereux

Airstrip

VMF-211

VMF-211

Commander Cunningham's command post, December 14–23

Contractors' aid station, December 12–23

Major Devereux's command post, December 14–23

Army Communication Unit, December 14–23

1DB aid station, December 12–23

3in. antiboat gun ("Hanna's Gun")

N

1. Initial position.
2. Second position.
3. Third position.

3in. or 5in. gun.
Searchlight.
.50-cal antiaircraft machine gun.
Active .30-cal machine-gun section.
Unmanned .30-cal machine-gun section.
Reinforced underground shelter.

1,500yds
1,000m

1DB · A

1DB · E

1DB · E

1DB · E

1DB · B

1DB · D

1DB · D

1DB · F

1DB · L

II 1DB · Devereux

Devereux

1DB

Raymond "Cap" Rutledge, one of the CPNAB volunteers, seen here as a POW in Shanghai, January 1942. He had served in the US Army during World War I, and as part of the mobile reserve he, along with Lt. Poindexter, threw hand grenades into the Japanese landing craft off Wake in the pre-dawn fighting of December 23. (USMC)

On 26 August 1941, Admiral Kimmel was able to report:

There are now at Wake twelve 3" AA guns, six 5" guns, eighteen .50 caliber AA machine guns, thirty .30 caliber machine guns, six searchlights and 176 defense battalion personnel. The emplacement of five inch guns is underway and, when installation of two of these guns is completed, the garrison will be capable of manning and operating four 3" AA guns, two 5" guns, eight .50 caliber AA machine guns, eight .30 caliber machine guns and three searchlights. It is contemplated that in a sudden emergency civilian personnel, which includes a considerable number of ex-service men, will augment the efforts of the Marines.

Although not substantial, it was a start.

The *Regulus* arrived off Wake on August 19, 1941, and the next day started loading the 1st Defense Battalion men and their equipment using the Marines as stevedores. The first job for the Marines was to establish their "tent city" on the site of the CPNAB original camp, Camp 1. The Marines next went to work emplacing the 5in. and 3in. antiaircraft guns around the islands. The three 5in. coastal batteries (of two guns each) were dispersed, with one for each of the three islands: Battery A at Peacock Point on Wake proper, Battery B to Toki Point on Peale Island, and Battery L to Kuku Point on Wilkes Island. The 5in. coastal guns had fixed mounts, as they were intended to be fitted to warships, and each mount required a pit 16ft by 16ft by 5ft deep (5m by 5m by 1.5m). The 12 3in. antiaircraft guns were similarly positioned in three four-gun batteries, again with one battery per island, positioned close to the 5in. guns in order to receive protection from aerial assault. Battery E was assigned to Wake proper, Battery D to Peale Island, and Battery F to Wilkes Island. Unlike the 5in. guns, the 3in. antiaircraft guns were on wheeled mounts, and as such could be redeployed if required (this would happen several times during the siege).

Major Hohn worked his men five and a half days a week on the defense works, from 0600hrs until 1730hrs, with one and a half hours off for lunch at the hottest time of the day. This was back-breaking work, even for the physically fit Marines, as nearly all of it was done by hand.

On September 30 the *Regulus* delivered two Navy officers and nine ratings, the advance guard for NAS (Naval Air Station) Wake Island. With nothing for them to do until the station was built, these men were ordered attached to 1st Defense Battalion, making a total of 184 military personnel on Wake.

On October 9 the USS *William Ward Burrows* arrived off Wake. On board was the 1st Defense Battalion's commanding officer and Maj. Hohn's replacement, Maj. Devereux. Major Hohn returned to Pearl Harbor on the *William Ward Burrows* on October 14. With Devereux's arrival on Wake things changed rapidly: he did everything by the book and practically no one in the 1st Defense Battalion liked him (it was said that his initials J. P. S. stood for "Just Plain Shit"). But Devereux knew his job and did it well. Work picked up, with Devereux working his men 12–14 hours per day including weekends; he rightly suspected that time was running out to prepare Wake for war.

At the end of October 1941, Devereux received reinforcements of eight officers and 194 enlisted men from 1st Defense Battalion, commanded by Major George Potter, who would become the battalion executive officer under Devereux. Major Devereux also initiated Admiral Kimmel's suggestion to instruct CPNAB volunteers in the use of the defense weapons. Some of these volunteers would serve with distinction during the siege. Some 200 CPNAB workers had volunteered.

The USS *Enterprise* delivered VMF-211's 12 F4F Wildcats to Wake four days prior to the outbreak of hostilities with Japan, which prevented it being sunk at Pearl Harbor. (NARA)

On November 28, 1941, the USS *Wright* began unloading its cargo and passengers onto Wake. Aboard were 43 naval personnel for the forthcoming Naval Air Station and 50 Marine ground crew from VMF-211, including Major Walter Bayler, with orders to establish an air–ground radio station for the incoming VMF-211 planes.

Also aboard the *Wright* was Cdr. Cunningham, the new island commander. One of Cdr. Cunningham's first directives as island commander was to place Maj. Devereux in charge of base defenses. Cunningham also placed VMF-211 at Devereux's disposal.

On December 4, 1941, Maj. Putnam landed his 12 F4F-3 Wildcats onto Wake's airstrip from on board the carrier *Enterprise*. These 12 planes would be the only air support Wake would have throughout the siege. So, at the outbreak of hostilities with Japan on December 8, 1941 (Wake time), the total number of defenders at Cdr. Cunningham's disposal for the defense of the atoll was as follows:

Unit name	Strength of unit
1st Defense Battalion	15 officers, 373 enlisted men
VMF-211	12 officers, 49 enlisted men
US Naval Air Station Wake Island	Ten officers, 58 ratings (without arms)
USS *Triton* (submarine)	One enlisted man, who had been landed for medical attention (without arms)
Army Air Corps	One officer, five enlisted men (without arms)
CPNAB volunteers	300–320 men (without arms)

JAPANESE FORCES

First landing, December 11, 1941

For the capture of Wake, Rear Admiral Kajioka had planned for three days of aerial assault from G3M twin-engine bombers of Air Flotilla 24. Kajioka sailed from his base on Kwajalein with his invasion task force on December 8, 1941, the same day that the aerial assault on Wake Island started. The invasion force itself consisted of Kajioka's Destroyer Squadron 6

(COMDESRON 6) with the light cruiser *Yubari* as his flagship, along with six destroyers: the *Mutsuki*, *Kisaragi*, *Yayoi*, *Mochizuki*, *Oite*, and *Hayate*. He also had with him two old destroyers that had been converted to carry assault troops – the *Aoi* and *Hagi* – and Daihatsu landing craft, these being redesignated as *Patrol Boat 32* and *Patrol Boat 33*. Also part of the invasion force were two armed merchantmen, *Kongo Maru* and *Kinryu Maru*, each carrying two Aichi E13A1 reconnaissance seaplanes in addition to troops and equipment for the assault. Ahead of the invasion force, three submarines – *RO65*, *RO66*, and *RO67* – were to reconnoiter Wake and be a guide for the invasion force.

Kajioka had additional gunfire support from the cruisers *Tatsuta* and *Tenryu* from the 18th Cruiser Division. Landing-force troops came from the 2nd Maizuru SNLF, the IJN's equivalent of the US Marine Corps. The plan called for 150 troops to land on Wilkes Island from *Mutsuki* and *Patrol Boat 33*, commanded by Special Duty Lieutenant (junior grade) Yakichi Itaya. A total of 300 troops would land on Wake proper in the *Oite* and *Patrol Boat 32*, commanded by Lieutenant Kinichi Uchida. If needed, the destroyers would provide additional men as landing-force troops.

Second landing, December 23, 1941

With the failure of the first attempted landings on Wake being blamed mainly on bad weather forcing the invasion fleet to abandon their landing attempts and retire back to Kwajalein, Admiral Inoue assembled a much greater force for the second attempt. Again, Rear Admiral Kajioka would be in overall command.

Kajioka's plans still called for landing-force troops to land on Wilkes Island and Wake proper's southern beaches, but this time without any preliminary naval bombardment, only a diversionary bombardment of Peale Island by the *Tenryu* and *Tatsuta*. Kajioka planned to land his troops, the first of two waves, under cover of darkness from landing craft and by beaching *Patrol Boat 32* and *Patrol Boat 33*. Some 900 troops would form the first wave, made up of rifle platoons as well as elements from the 2nd SNLF antiaircraft unit, company headquarters, and heavy-weapons unit.

Kajioka's second wave would consist of 1,100 troops, a mixed force of SNLF troops and "bluejacket" (naval) infantry. These would land after daybreak wherever they were most required. Kajioka had also once again given orders to issue arms to the destroyer crews and land them as additional infantry if needed. Also aboard *Patrol Boat 32* were 70 men of the Kesshitai ("Do or die force"), commanded by Warrant Officer Kiroku Horie. This force was to land on Wake proper, west of Peacock Point, and push northward to the airfield and Wake's command center.

All this was to be supported, after daybreak, by aircraft from the *Hiryu* and *Soryu*. The invasion force's orders were to "seize Wake at all costs."

A sample of handguns used by the IJN. (Top left) 8mm ("Papa") Nambu Type 14 with lanyard, and large modified trigger guard; (bottom left) improved 1904 Nambu, with Navy anchor marking; (center) 9mm Type 26 revolver; (top right) 8mm Type 94; (bottom right) imported 7.65mm Fabrique Nationale/Browning M1910. (Steve Hayama)

ORDERS OF BATTLE

US FORCES

NAVAL FORCES

Commandant 14th Naval District

    Admiral Husband E. Kimmel (December 8–17, 1941)

    Vice Admiral William Pye (December 17–31, 1941)

Pacific Fleet, Task Group 7.2

    USS *Triton*

    USS *Tambor*

Pacific Fleet, Task Force 14 (Wake Island relief force)

    Task Force Commander – Rear Admiral Jack Fletcher

    USS *Saratoga* with VMF-221 on board

    Cruiser Division 6 – *Astoria, Minneapolis,* and *San Francisco*

    Nine destroyers

    Seaplane tender *Tangier*

    Fleet oiler *Neches*

    4th Defense Battalion, with nine officers and 201 enlisted men (including one officer and four corpsmen of the USN)

    VMF-221 ground crew

Island Commander Wake

    Commander Winfield Scott Cunningham, USN

Naval Air Base Wake

    Commander Campbell Keene, USN

    Ten officers, 58 ratings

Navy contract NOY 4173

    Resident Officer-in-Charge – Lt. Cdr. Elmer B. Greey, USNR

    1,200 CPNAB construction workers (Dan Teters as superintendent)

MARINE FORCES (MAJ. JAMES DEVEREUX)

1st Defense Battalion

Headquarters

    Commanding officer – Maj. James Devereux

    Executive officer – Maj. George H. Potter

    Munitions officer – Marine Gunner John Hamas

    Ordnance officer – Marine Gunner Harold C. Borth

    Medical officer – Lt. Kahn, USN

Wilkes Strongpoint (Capt. Platt)

    Ordnance and maintenance (Gunner McKinstry)

    Battery G – six 60in. searchlights, less four detached

    Battery L – two 5in. guns (2nd Lt. McAlister)

    Battery F – four 3in. antiaircraft guns (no personnel assigned and no fire control equipment)

Wake Peacock Point Strongpoint (1st Lt. Barninger)

    Battery A – two 5in. guns (1st Lt. Barninger)

    Battery E – four 3in. antiaircraft guns (1st Lt. Lewis)

    Four .50-cal machine guns

    Four .30-cal machine guns

Peale Strongpoint (Capt. Godbold)

    Battery B – two 5in. guns (1st Lt. Kessler)

    Four .50-cal machine guns

    Four .30-cal machine guns

    Battery D – four 3in. antiaircraft guns, with personnel for three guns (Capt. Godbold)

    Battery H – 18 .50-cal machine guns, less 12 detached (2nd Lt. Hanna)

    Battery I – 30 .30-cal machine guns, less 14 detached (2nd Lt. Poindexter)

Mobile reserve (Lt. Poindexter)

    Four .30-cal machine guns

    Administration and supply personnel serving as infantry (approximately 80 men)

VMF-211 (Maj. Paul A. Putnam)

    12 F4F-3 Wildcats

    Service-and-supply unit (12 officers, 29 enlisted men)

US ARMY AIR CORPS

    Radio Operations Group (Capt. Henry S. Wilson)

    Five enlisted men

CPNAB VOLUNTEERS

    300–320 men

JAPANESE FORCES

2ND MAIZURU SPECIAL NAVAL LANDING FORCE (SNLF)

Force headquarters
Commander
Executive officer
Warrant officer
46 enlisted men

1st and 2nd Companies
HQ Platoon – one officer, 35 enlisted men
1st, 2nd, 3rd, 4th Rifle Platoons – one officer, 50 enlisted men per platoon
Heavy Machine Gun Platoon – one officer, 55 enlisted men

Heavy-weapons unit
Eight officers, 212 enlisted men
Regimental Gun HQ – one officer, 16 enlisted men
1st and 2nd Regimental Gun Platoons – one officer, 50 enlisted men each
Battalion Howitzer HQ – one officer, 16 enlisted men
1st and 2nd Battalion Howitzer Platoons – one officer, 40 enlisted men each

Communications unit
One officer, 18 enlisted men

Engineer unit
One officer, nine enlisted men

Medical unit
Three officers, 33 enlisted men

Supply unit
Two officers, 53 enlisted men

Transportation unit
One officer, 51 enlisted men

Total personnel
11 officers
25 warrant officers
1,033 enlisted men
1,069 total

FORCES FOR SEIZURE OF WAKE, DECEMBER 8–13, 1941

Commander-in-Chief 4th Fleet Vice Admiral Inoue

Air Flotilla 24
Air Attack Force 1
34 G3M-2 Type 96 Navy bombers
Air Attack Force 3
Seven Kawanishi H6K4 Type 97 flying boats

Destroyer Squadron 6
Cruiser *Yubari* (Rear Admiral Kajioka's flagship)
Six destroyers – *Mutsuki, Kisaragi, Yayoi, Mochizuki, Oite,* and *Hayate*
Patrol Boat 32 and *Patrol Boat 33*
Armed merchantmen – *Kongo Maru* and *Kinryu Maru*
Reconnaissance Division – submarines *RO-65, RO-66,* and *RO-67*

Covering Support Force
18th Cruiser Division (Rear Admiral Marumo) – *Tatsuta* and *Tenryu*

6th Base Force (occupation troops to be used as additional assault-force troops if required)
65th Naval Ground Unit
4th Naval Pioneer Unit

2nd Maizuru SNLF
450 officers and men under the command of Lt. Uchida and Special Duty Lt. Itaya.

FORCES FOR THE SEIZURE OF WAKE, DECEMBER 23, 1941

This force was the same as that above, with the following additional units:

Reinforcement force
8th Cruiser Division –*Tone* and *Chikuma*
2nd Carrier Division – *Hiryu* and *Soryu*
The destroyers *Tanikaze* and *Urakaze*
The armed merchantmen *Kiyokawa Maru* and *Tenyo Maru*
Two additional destroyers from the 24th Destroyer Division (to replace the sunken *Kisaragi* and *Hayate*)

Additional landing-force troops
2nd Maizuru SNLF – HQ company (Itaya)
Antiaircraft Platoon, Land Force HQ (Tanaka)
Machine-gun platoon
Kesshitai – "Do or die force" (Horie)
Takano – "100 picked men"

OPPOSING PLANS

US PLANS

By 1940 the strategic importance of Wake as a naval base was considerable to the US Navy. In 1938 the Hepburn Report saw Wake as being of such importance that it recommended a budget of $7,600,000 for a three-year base-development program, intended to transform Wake into an advance base for LRP (long-range patrol) aircraft reconnaissance and a secondary role as an intermediate station on the air route to the Far East. The report went on to say that "The immediate continuous operations of patrol planes from Wake would be vital at the outbreak of war in the Pacific."

In response to the Hepburn Report, work commenced on turning Wake into a naval advance base in early 1941, starting with the construction of base facilities, but with no immediate thoughts toward base defense. Not until April 1941, with the advent of Admiral Kimmel's report to the CNO, was serious consideration given to Wake's defense capabilities. As a result, on June 23, 1941, orders were issued directing elements of the 1st Defense Battalion to be established at Wake.

A USMC F4F Wildcat, seen here at Henderson Field. This was the aircraft flown by the pilots of VMF-211 during the defense of Wake Island. The Wildcat was popular because of its durability and reliability, being able to take great punishment and still bring the pilot home in one piece. (US Navy)

Major Devereux's Marines were hampered in their defensive preparations by having the Army use Wake as a staging post for the refueling of flights of B17 Flying Fortresses en route to the Philippines. All these aircraft had to be refueled by the Marines, basically by hand, as there was only one fuelling truck on the atoll. There were no Army Air Force (AAF) personnel on Wake except for an Army Airways Communication Service radio van, manned by a captain and five enlisted men. These flights could descend upon Wake any time of day or night and would require immediate attention from the Marines to get them on their way as quickly as possible.

Major Putnam had received secret verbal orders from Commander Aircraft Battle Force on November 27 to prepare to transfer his 12 F4F Wildcats of VMF-211 from Ewa Mooring Mast base on Hawaii to a carrier. The 12 aircraft had flown from Ewa to the naval airbase on Ford Island in the middle of Pearl Harbor and on November 28 transferred to the carrier USS *Enterprise*.

On the morning of December 4, 1941, led in by a Navy PBY patrol seaplane sent out from Wake, the 12 F4F-3 Wildcats of VMF-211 took off from the carrier USS *Enterprise* and landed safely on the new airstrip on Wake. They would be the only air support Wake would have throughout the forthcoming battle. In a personal letter to his commanding officer back at Pearl Harbor, Colonel Claude A. Larkin, Major Putnam best described his feelings for the voyage and plans for the future of VMF-211. Below is the letter reproduced in its entirety, which was written by Putnam on the eve of VMF-211's departure from the *Enterprise* onto Wake:

At Sea
December 3, 1941

Dear Colonel Larkin:

It is expected that we will go ashore tomorrow morning. The extreme secrecy under which we sailed is still in effect and I understand is to remain so at least until this Force has returned to the Hawaiian operating area. Therefore I am sending this first report via guard mail on this ship, rather than by air mail after landing.

In the absence of instructions, it is my intention to send data for muster and pay rolls direct to the squadron for inclusion by the first sergeant in his routine reports; normal requisitions to supply will go via your office except "rush" and emergency matter which I have been instructed by ComAirBatFor [Commander Aircraft Battle Force] to handle in what seems at the time to be the most direct and effective manner and let the paper work catch up later; and reports of conditions and activities (and my weeping) will be by informal letter to you. I will of course appreciate any suggestions or instructions that you may have for me.

You will recall that I left one plane at Ford Island. The Admiral at once gave me a plane to replace it, from VF-6; and he made it plain to me and to the whole ship that nothing should be overlooked nor any trouble spared in order to insure that I will get ashore with 12 airplanes in as near perfect condition as possible. Immediately I was given a full complement of mechs [mechanics] and all hands aboard have continually vied with each other to see who could do the most for me. I feel a bit like the fatted calf being groomed for whatever it is that happens to fatted calves, but it surely is nice while it lasts

The Japanese carrier *Hiryu*. Along with carrier *Soryu*, it was diverted from its return from the attack on Pearl Harbor to provide air support to Rear Admiral Kajioka's second attempt to invade Wake Island, on December 23, 1941. (NARA)

and the airplanes are pretty sleek and fat too. They have of course been checked and double checked from end to end, and they have also been painted so that all 12 are now of standard blue and gray.

I have no information as to where the WRIGHT put Conderman and my "yellow ball" [aircraft maintenance] materiel ashore. That's one of those things that may have to be handled in the most direct and effective manner.

The Admiral seems to be most determined to maintain secrecy regarding the position and activity of this Force. There has been a continuous inner air patrol during daylight, and a full squadron has made a long search to the front and flanks each morning and evening. They are armed to the teeth and the orders are to attack any Japanese vessel or aircraft on sight in order to prevent the discovery of this Force.

My orders, however, are not so direct. In fact I have no orders. I have been told informally by lesser members of Staff that I will be given orders only to fly off the ship and go to the land, and that there will be nothing in the way of instructions other than to do what seems appropriate at the moment. Of course I shall go and ask for orders and instructions, but it seems unlikely that I shall be given anything definite. What's the price on starting a war these days? They seem to be quite plentiful this season, so the price has probably fallen off a bit, one way of the other.

The Japanese light cruiser *Tenryu* was one of the oldest cruisers still in service in the IJN in 1942, having been built in 1919. It was attacked by the Wildcats of VMF-211, but suffered no crippling damage. (Yamato Museum)

This is written Wednesday forenoon. Should I receive any orders at variance with the foregoing, I will add a postscript. Otherwise I think of nothing further of importance or interest at this time.

Respectfully,
P. A. Putnam

P.S. The matter of secrecy seems to be still in effect. Suggest that Comdr. Browning be consulted before releasing any of the enclosed information which might indicate whereabouts.
P. A. P.

Upon arriving at Wake, Maj. Putnam reported to the island commander, Cdr. Cunningham, for orders. He then toured the landing strip and aviation area with Major Bayler and Lieutenant Conderman and was alarmed at the lack of facilities for his aircraft and personnel. Only the main landing strip was operational; the secondary strip was still under construction and the main landing strip was only wide enough to permit landing and takeoff by single aircraft. Parking space was extremely restricted, and the areas outside the parking mats were so rough and uneven that any attempt to use them to disperse any planes on the ground would result in serious damage to the aircraft. Fueling operations were still generally carried out manually.

No aircraft revetments or shelters existed as yet, a matter that Maj. Putnam immediately raised with Cdr. Cunningham. Major Putnam's orders from Cdr. Cunningham were to commence dawn and dusk patrols of four aircraft as soon as was practical. This Putnam did, including training his pilots and ground crews with their unfamiliar new planes, starting from December 6. On the eve of war with Japan, Wake was far from ready, with the civilian contractors and men of the Naval Construction Unit working on base facilities and the airstrip, and only the Marines of the 1st Defense Battalion and VMF-211 working on the island's defenses. PanAm even continued their clipper service, and although everyone on Wake was fully aware of the worsening situation with Japan, the news from Pearl Harbor on Monday December 8, 1941 (December 7 at Pearl Harbor), still came as a shock.

JAPANESE PLANS

The American presence on Wake had not gone unnoticed by the Japanese, and when in March of 1935 the US Secretary of the Navy, Claude Swanson, announced that he had given permission to PanAm to establish aviation facilities on Guam, Midway, and Wake for their clipper service to China and the Philippines, Japan's naval authorities registered their disapproval in a strongly worded article in the Japanese press, declaring that the proposed landing places could quickly be converted into naval bases and as such posed a potential danger to Japan and her "mandated island." Japan further considered the US moves to be "a problem requiring serious consideration." Japan's fears of a US naval build-up on Wake were heightened further by the presence of US Navy Corps of Civil Engineers personnel, who carried out detailed surveys of the atoll.

Naval situation around Wake Island, December 8–23, 1941

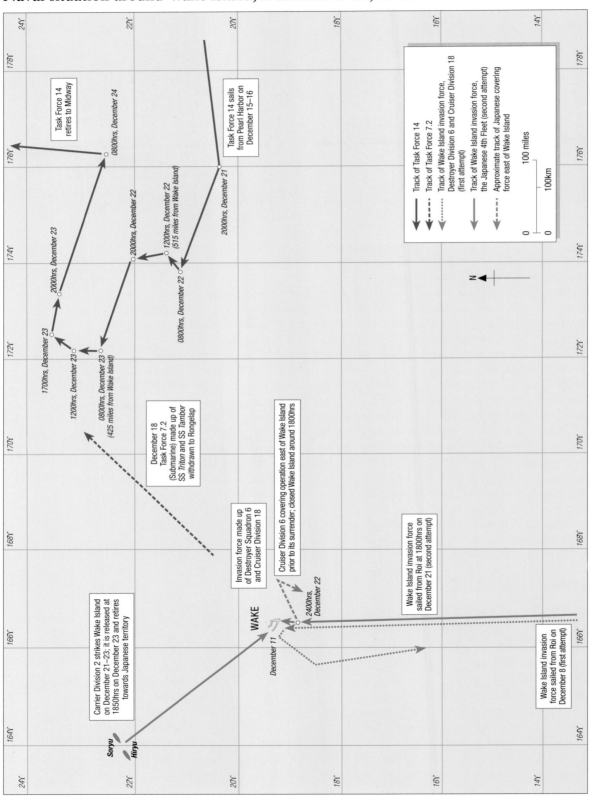

Task Force 14 retires to Midway

0800hrs, December 24

Task Force 14 sails from Pearl Harbor on December 15–16

2000hrs, December 23

2000hrs, December 23

2000hrs, December 22

1200hrs, December 22

1200hrs, December 22 (515 miles from Wake Island)

2000hrs, December 21

0800hrs, December 22

1700hrs, December 23

1200hrs, December 23

0800hrs, December 23 (425 miles from Wake Island)

December 18 Task Force 7.2 (Submarine) made up of SS Triton and SS Tambor withdrawn to Rongelap

Invasion force made up of Destroyer Squadron 6 and Cruiser Division 18

Cruiser Division 6 covering operation east of Wake Island prior to its surrender; closed Wake Island around 1800hrs

2400hrs, December 22

Carrier Division 2 strikes Wake Island on December 21–23; it is released at 1850hrs on December 23 and retires towards Japanese territory

WAKE

December 11

Wake Island invasion force sailed from Roi at 1800hrs on December 21 (second attempt)

Wake Island invasion force sailed from Roi on December 8 (first attempt)

Soryu

Hiryu

N

Key

Track of Task Force 14

Track of Task Force 7.2

Track of Wake Island invasion force, Destroyer Division 6 and Cruiser Division 18 (first attempt)

Track of Wake Island invasion force, the Japanese 4th Fleet (second attempt)

Approximate track of Japanese covering force east of Wake Island

0   100 miles

0   100km

PanAm works continued on Wake under the watchful eyes of the Japanese and, with the commencement of US Navy construction works, Japan realized that Wake must be taken in the event of all-out war with the United States.

Japanese war plans were formulated as early as 1938, in the top-secret "East Asia War Plan." In this extensive document, which laid out the requirement of establishing Japan's new outer-defense perimeter, the capture of Wake Island was a key objective for the IJN's 4th Fleet.

The 4th Fleet's commander, Admiral Inoue, gave the task of capturing Wake to Rear Admiral Kajioka. Kajioka's plans called for an initial aerial bombardment; this would be carried out by the 4th Fleet's air wing of bombers from the 24th Air Flotilla, based at Roi and Majuro. The air assault would commence the same day as the attack on Pearl Harbor. The invasion force, designated as "COMDESRON 6," consisting of a covering and support force of cruisers and destroyers, the 6th Base Force, and 450 SNLF troops. Not considered to be an overwhelming invasion force (there was no carrier ground-support group), this force was considered by Admiral Inoue to be "adequate." The invasion force was to sortie out of Kwajalein on December 8, the same day as the start of the aerial assault on Wake, and was expected to arrive off Wake on December 11.

Kajioka's landing plan was to land 150 SNLF troops on the southern shore of Wilkes Island, and a further 300 SNLF troops on the southern shore of Wake proper to capture the airstrip. In the event of stiff resistance, Kajioka could call upon the crews of the invasion fleet and land them as "bluejacket" infantry.

LEFT
A 5in. gun. Six of these were the main defense weapons on Wake. Note the sentry kitted out in obsolete World War I equipment and weaponry. (Author's collection)

RIGHT
An aerial view of Wake, taken in December 2009. At the center is the northern leg of Wake proper and at center right is Peale Island. In the distance is the southern leg of Wake proper and Wilkes Island. (Author's photo)

THE BATTLE OF WAKE ISLAND

A DATE THAT WILL LIVE IN INFAMY

Sunday, December 7, 1941, dawned bright and clear for the men on Wake. The day before, Maj. Devereux had held a practice general drill for his Marines, the first he had been able to conduct because of the much more pressing requirements of preparing the island's defenses. The drill ran so smoothly that Maj. Devereux ordered that the men could have the rest of Saturday off as leisure time and that Sunday was to be holiday routine. So the men on Wake did laundry, cleaned barrack tents, slept, or wrote letters, some thinking about the rest of the 1st Defense Battalion Marines still languishing in comparative luxury back on Hawaii. But on Hawaii, on the other side of the International Date Line to Wake, it was still Saturday December 6.

In 1941, USMC and Army personnel still wore the M1917 helmet, or "Brodie helmet," used during World War I. This helmet was designed to protect against shell bursts exploding overhead, hence the wide brim. It would be replaced by the M1 helmet in 1942.

Monday December 8 started with reveille at 0600hrs as usual for the Marines, the start of yet another grueling 12–14 hours of back-breaking work on Wake's defenses. Breakfast was being served to the Marines in Camp 1, and to the civilian contractors and Army and Navy personnel at Camp 2. The Army Airways Communication Service radio van was manned as usual, ready to receive any communication from Hickam Field on Oahu of any B17 flights to the Philippines. What the radio operator, Sergeant Rex, received over his headset made him sit up in disbelief. A frantic, uncoded, procedureless transmission came through his headset in Morse code, which he relayed to his commanding officer, Captain Wilson. The message was as clear as it was unbelievable: "SOS, SOS, Japs attacking Oahu. This is the real thing. No mistake."

Captain Wilson ordered Sgt. Rex to obtain as many details as possible whilst he rushed the news to Maj. Devereux. Almost at the same time as Maj. Devereux was receiving the news from Capt. Wilson, Cdr. Cunningham was leaving the contractors' mess hall with several of his Navy officers, to be confronted with a breathless messenger from the Navy communication office that they had received a frantic message: "Pearl Harbor under attack from Japanese planes. This is no drill! Repeat – this is no drill."

Major Devereux tried unsuccessfully to contact Cdr. Cunningham by telephone (Cunningham was on his way to Devereux by pickup truck) and so he called for the field music (bugler) on watch and ordered him to sound "Call to Arms." On hearing the bugle call, the Marines dropped everything and ran back to their tents to collect helmets, arms and ammunition and mounted trucks, which rushed them to their gun positions. By 0745hrs all gun positions had telephoned in to Devereux's command post reporting that they were manned and ready.

Because of the low-lying terrain on Wake and the lack of any radar, the only advance warning possible to the defenders on Wake would come from the two men manning an improvised lookout point on Wake, on top of the water tower at Camp 1. Cunningham had previously instructed Maj. Putnam to have four-plane dawn and dusk patrols out. The dawn patrol was already airborne when the word from Pearl Harbor was received. Cunningham also contacted PanAm's airport manager, John Cooke, requesting him to recall the clipper, at this time only 10 minutes out of Wake. This he did, using a pre-arranged code message: "CASE SEVEN, CONDITION A."

Lieutenant Commander Greey telephoned CPNAB Superintendent Dan Teters, telling him of the events on Oahu and that a state of war now existed between US and Japan. Teters went to his office and conferred with Cdr. Cunningham and Lt. Cdr. Greey; it was agreed that Teters and his construction

This composite photograph shows the USS *Enterprise* in October 1941, with waves of aircraft superimposed above the carrier. The men and aircraft of VMF-211 were transported to Wake Island aboard this vessel, arriving there on December 4, 1941. (US National Archives)

The USS *Arizona* burns after being attacked by Japanese aircraft during the attack on Pearl Harbor. Occurring more or less simultaneously with the strike on Wake, the attack finally pushed the US into joining World War II. (NARA)

teams would continue with their scheduled construction work. Teters then contacted Maj. Devereux, who asked him to turn over the civilians who had volunteered to assist in the island's defenses to his command.

Cunningham next went to the airstrip to confer with Maj. Putnam with regard to the dispersal and protection of VMF-211's precious aircraft. Having arrived on Wake only four days previously, one of which had been a holiday, VMF-211 had barely had time to unpack, let alone have the airstrip ready for a state of war. Only the main runway was operational, as the secondary runways were still under construction. There was a small parking area but the ground beyond prevented any possibility of dispersing the planes further. Men and machines from CPNAB were hastily constructing dispersal revetments, but these would not be in a fit state to receive aircraft until about 1400hrs. Major Putnam was faced with the choice of moving the planes now over rough terrain to disperse them further from aerial attack, risking almost certain damage, or wait until the revetments were complete. Unfortunately for the planes on the ground, Maj. Putnam made the wrong choice in leaving the planes where they were. The pilots and ground crews of VMF-211 spent the morning dispersing the eight Wildcats on the parking area as best they could whilst they hastily armed them to be ready for action. They also relocated the squadron radio installation alongside the runway to an area farther into the brush, and sandbagged and camouflaged it.

As an act of defiance, at 0800hrs Maj. Devereux ordered his field music to sound "Morning Colors" as the Stars and Stripes was hoisted aloft. All over Wake, defense preparations were being carried out at a fever pitch throughout the morning, and trucks were racing around dropping off 5in. and 3in. ammunition as well as cases of machine-gun ammunition, small-arms ammunition, and hand grenades. From the storeroom at Camp 1 the Marines issued what few additional small arms they had to the unarmed Navy bluejackets and the Army radio group.

Everyone not manning the various gun positions was involved with digging slit trenches and filling sandbags. Major Devereux informed Cdr. Cunningham that he was moving his command post from his tent at Camp 1 to an underground dugout in the brush east of Camp 1, and Cdr. Cunningham informed Maj. Devereux that he would maintain his command post at his temporary office at Camp 2. The VMF-211 command post remained in the squadron tent at the airstrip.

Having returned from the dawn patrol at 0900hrs, Maj. Putnam ordered four planes airborne at all times, and for the remaining eight planes to be readied for immediate takeoff. The four planes aloft were to patrol to the north and south of Wake, with the south being the direction from which Wake expected an aerial attack. That done, Maj. Putnam left the airstrip to confer with Cdr. Cunningham and the PanAm clipper pilot with regards to a long-range reconnaissance patrol using the clipper escorted by two Wildcats from VMF-211. This patrol was scheduled to take off at 1300hrs. Putnam then returned to the airstrip to ready the two-plane escort.

At 12,000ft (3,660m), having finished their patrol to the south of Wake, the combat air patrol swung north. Unbeknown to them, half a mile beneath them below the clouds, were 34 G3M bombers of Air Attack Force 1 of the 24th Air Flotilla. They had taken off at dawn from their base at Roi, 720 miles (1,160km) to the south of Wake, and were commanded by Lieutenant Commander Matsuda Hideo. Matsuda ordered the three waves of bombers to drop to 10,000ft (3,048m) for their final bombing run on Wake, but observing that Wake's southern shores were almost obscured by a rain squall at about 2,000ft (610m), Matsuda ordered his bombers to drop into the tail of the rain squall and to cut their motors to quieten their approach further. This they did and the bombers emerged through the rain a few seconds later, just before noon, directly over Wake's airstrip and totally undetected by Wake's defenders. At 1158hrs, 1st Lieutenant Lewis, commanding Battery E

This general view of Wake Island shows the kind of terrain that the combatants fought over. Once off the beach, thick scrub made movement and observation difficult. (Getty)

Situation on Wake Island and Wilkes Island, 1300–0400hrs, December 23, 1941

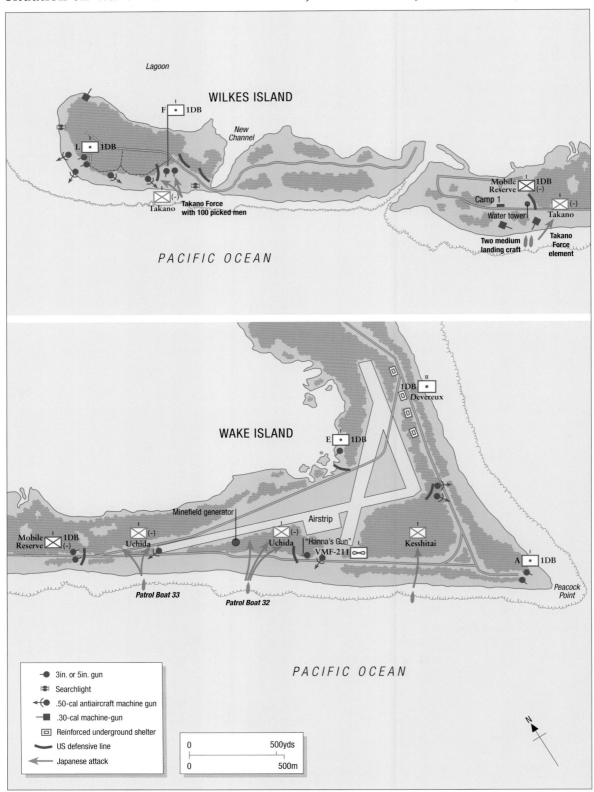

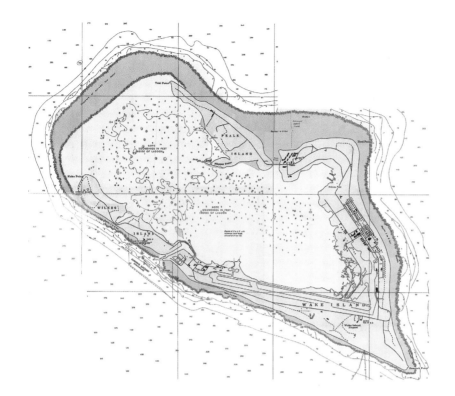

Current-day map of Wake. Little has changed other than the airstrip being extended and tarmac roads replacing the crushed-coral roadways. The wooden bridge connecting Wake and Peale was lost in the last typhoon to hit Wake Island and as yet has not been rebuilt. Wilkes is now a nature reserve and uninhabited; the only people on the atoll are construction crews and administration personnel for the airport for the occasional emergency or military flight. Access is still restricted.

at Peacock Point, looked skyward to see a "V" of 12 aircraft heading over between Camp 1 and Peacock Point, and grabbed the field telephone connected to Devereux's command post. Bright sparks began to fill the air from the incendiary and tracer bullets from the strafing planes. Lewis had two of his four guns manned and ready and within seconds they opened up on the bombers, using data estimated by Lewis, as Battery E had no height finder, in addition to the .50-cal machine guns around the airstrip. The Japanese bombers knew their job well and carried out a textbook "checkerboard" bombing of the airstrip area with 100lb fragmentation bombs as well as 20mm incendiary bullets. One of the two other "Vs" of G3M bombers bombed and strafed Camp 2, and the other swung back to approach Camp 1 and the airstrip area from the west before turning northwest, heading for the PanAm installations on Peale, which received similar treatment. By 1210hrs the Japanese bombers had expended all their bombs and ammunition and so they climbed to a cruising altitude and headed back to base, waggling their wings to signify "Banzai." Although considerable flak had been put up by Batteries E and D, and also by .50-cal machine guns, the Japanese lost no planes, though several were hit and at least one crew member was killed.

The combat air patrol, without air–ground communications and patrolling at a high altitude to the north of Wake, was oblivious to the disaster down on the ground. Two of the Wildcats had swung southeast and climbed to 13,000ft (3,962m) to avoid the overcast skies and were returning to Wake when one of the pilots, 2nd Lieutenant Kinney, spotted two formations of bombers below in the distance. As they broke through the clouds, the two Marine pilots, 2nd Lieutenant Kinney and Technical Sergeant Hamilton, saw oily black smoke rising from Wake. They raced after the retiring bombers, but lost them in clouds and returned to Wake. The other two Wildcats returned to Wake oblivious of what had happened until they landed.

On the ground it was a scene of utter devastation. Seven of the eight Wildcats that had been parked were completely destroyed. Two pilots, Lieutenants Graves and Holden, were killed outright; a third pilot, Lieutenant Conderman, was badly wounded and would die before daybreak the next day. The eighth Wildcat had been damaged but could be repaired. To add to the misfortunes of VMF-211, Captain Elrod on landing his plane struck his propeller on debris on the runway, making for a total of nine Wildcats out of action. On the airfield the air–ground radio installation that was being set up by Major Bayler was severely damaged and out of action. The 25,000-gallon Avgas tank had been hit, resulting in a sea of flames that engulfed the whole airstrip area; 50-gallon fuel drums were exploding and the squadron's tents containing their scant stock of tools and what few spare parts they had were ablaze. Worst of all, the squadron's aviation personnel had suffered over 60 percent casualties. In addition to the three pilots, 23 ground crew were killed outright or would die before morning the next day, and 11 more were wounded. Among the wounded were three more of the squadron's pilots: Maj. Putnam, Captain Tharin and Staff Sergeant Arthur.

Over the rest of Wake things were not much better. Camp 2 and the PanAm facilities, including the hotel and the seaplane facilities, had been badly damaged and were ablaze. Ten PanAm employees were dead. Amazingly, the clipper, although sustaining numerous bullet holes, had not been struck in any vital components. As such, it was loaded with its five passengers and 26 Caucasian employees (Cdr. Cunningham commenting later that he felt it to be "an unfortunate time to draw the color line") and successfully took off after several attempts, heading for Midway Island.

Over at Camp 2, the CPNAB contractors had suffered 25 dead and many more wounded. Damage control started immediately after the Japanese bombers had departed, with the main priority being the airstrip area. The wounded were transported to the CPNAB hospital at Camp 2, run by Dr Lawton Shank. The 1st Defense Battalion surgeon, Lieutenant Gustave Kahn (MC) USN, joined the doctor along with all available corpsmen. The dead were collected and put into a temporary mortuary, utilizing one of the cooler trailers at Camp 2.

Portable coincidence rangefinder. These were used in conjunction with the 5in. coastal-defense guns as part of Wake's defenses and, like the 5in. guns, were relics removed from decommissioned battleships. (USMC)

As soon as practicable the remaining three airworthy Wildcats were fueled, armed, and sent aloft, mainly to protect them from being caught on the ground by any further Japanese bombing.

Whilst the clear-up was going on Maj. Putnam set about the task of reorganizing his depleted squadron. Putnam had lost all his aviation mechanics, including his engineering officer 1st Lieutenant Graves, who had been killed in the bombing. Putnam appointed 2nd Lieutenant Kinney as his replacement, with Technical Sergeant Hamilton as principal assistant. Major Putnam promised Kinney "a medal as big as a pie" if he kept the few remaining Wildcats flying. Immediately Kinney and Hamilton with the help of some CPNAB and Navy mechanics sent over from Camp 2 set about salvaging anything they could from the wreckage. In addition, Maj. Putnam appointed Captain Freuler to reorganize the ordnance section, Lieutenant Kliewer the radio, and Captains Elrod and Tharin set about supervising the construction of foxholes, shelters, and infantry defensive works. Work on constructing revetments for the remaining planes continued, and work started on mining the airstrip with dynamite charges at 150ft (46m) intervals as an anti-airborne-assault measure. Additionally, all open ground around the airstrip had deep furrows plowed into it by bulldozers in order to prevent air-assault landings, and instructions were given that heavy construction equipment was to be parked overnight at intervals across the runway. Major Putnam agreed with Cdr. Cunningham to add a midday combat air patrol in addition to the dawn and dusk patrols, in view of the likelihood that Japanese bombers taking off from their Marshall Islands bases at dawn would arrive over Wake around noon.

All over the atoll, defensive works were being constructed at fever pitch. With the program of works for the Naval Air Station by the CPNAB contractors halted, many of the civilians took to hiding in the brush, though Dan Teters had over 300 volunteers willing to help the Marines in any way they could. This they did, some manning artillery pieces or machine-gun emplacements, some driving trucks distributing food and ammunition, and others operating machines digging foxholes and shelters. Throughout the night Lt. Kinney and his makeshift maintenance crew worked on the damaged Wildcats and was able to report by next morning that the squadron now had four airworthy aircraft.

LEFT
For antiair defense, water-cooled .50-cal machine guns were placed on M2A1 mounts. The water-cooled barrel allowed for long periods of sustained firing before the gun began to overheat. (NARA)

RIGHT
The view from the other side. These Japanese aviators in the cockpit of a 96 Rikko are eating a meal, as aircrew often did when they had to remain airborne for long periods. (Edward M. Young)

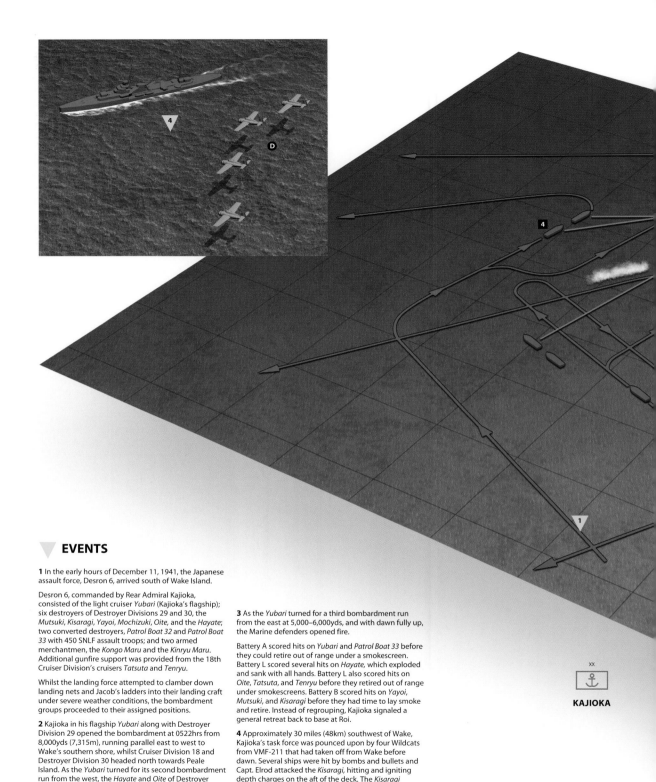

EVENTS

1 In the early hours of December 11, 1941, the Japanese assault force, Desron 6, arrived south of Wake Island.

Desron 6, commanded by Rear Admiral Kajioka, consisted of the light cruiser *Yubari* (Kajioka's flagship); six destroyers of Destroyer Divisions 29 and 30, the *Mutsuki, Kisaragi, Yayoi, Mochizuki, Oite,* and the *Hayate*; two converted destroyers, *Patrol Boat 32* and *Patrol Boat 33* with 450 SNLF assault troops; and two armed merchantmen, the *Kongo Maru* and the *Kinryu Maru*. Additional gunfire support was provided from the 18th Cruiser Division's cruisers *Tatsuta* and *Tenryu*.

Whilst the landing force attempted to clamber down landing nets and Jacob's ladders into their landing craft under severe weather conditions, the bombardment groups proceeded to their assigned positions.

2 Kajioka in his flagship *Yubari* along with Destroyer Division 29 opened the bombardment at 0522hrs from 8,000yds (7,315m), running parallel east to west to Wake's southern shore, whilst Cruiser Division 18 and Destroyer Division 30 headed north towards Peale Island. As the *Yubari* turned for its second bombardment run from the west, the *Hayate* and *Oite* of Destroyer Division 29 broke off and headed towards Wilkes Island.

3 As the *Yubari* turned for a third bombardment run from the east at 5,000–6,000yds, and with dawn fully up, the Marine defenders opened fire.

Battery A scored hits on *Yubari* and *Patrol Boat 33* before they could retire out of range under a smokescreen. Battery L scored several hits on *Hayate,* which exploded and sank with all hands. Battery L also scored hits on *Oite, Tatsuta,* and *Tenryu* before they retired out of range under smokescreens. Battery B scored hits on *Yayoi, Mutsuki,* and *Kisaragi* before they had time to lay smoke and retire. Instead of regrouping, Kajioka signaled a general retreat back to base at Roi.

4 Approximately 30 miles (48km) southwest of Wake, Kajioka's task force was pounced upon by four Wildcats from VMF-211 that had taken off from Wake before dawn. Several ships were hit by bombs and bullets and Capt. Elrod attacked the *Kisaragi,* hitting and igniting depth charges on the aft of the deck. The *Kisaragi* exploded and sank within minutes, with all hands lost.

KAJIOKA

ATTEMPTED JAPANESE LANDINGS, DECEMBER 11, 1941

The first Japanese attempt to capture Wake Island is repulsed, and suffers heavy losses.

Note: Gridlines are shown at intervals of 2km/2187yds

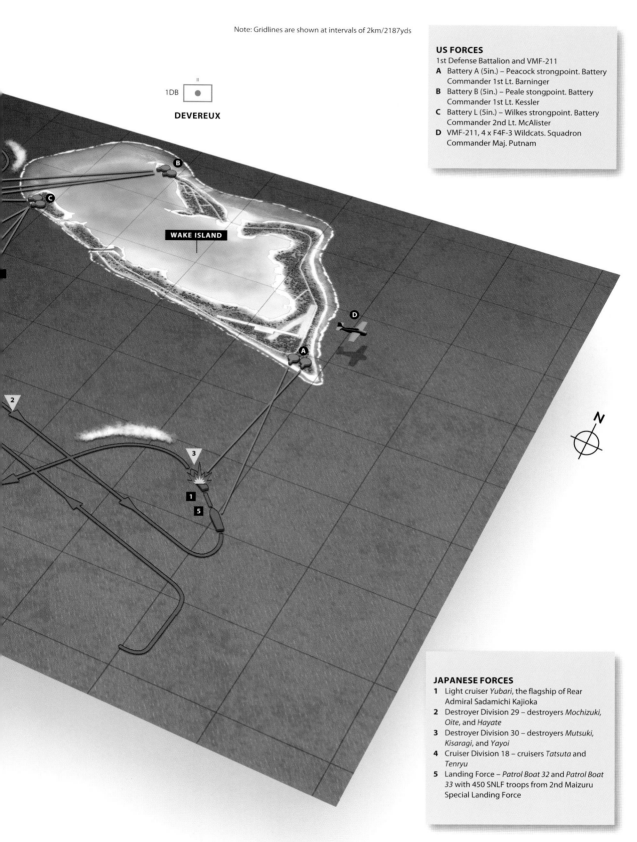

1DB
DEVEREUX

WAKE ISLAND

N

US FORCES
1st Defense Battalion and VMF-211
A Battery A (5in.) – Peacock strongpoint. Battery Commander 1st Lt. Barninger
B Battery B (5in.) – Peale stongpoint. Battery Commander 1st Lt. Kessler
C Battery L (5in.) – Wilkes strongpoint. Battery Commander 2nd Lt. McAlister
D VMF-211, 4 x F4F-3 Wildcats. Squadron Commander Maj. Putnam

JAPANESE FORCES
1 Light cruiser *Yubari*, the flagship of Rear Admiral Sadamichi Kajioka
2 Destroyer Division 29 – destroyers *Mochizuki, Oite,* and *Hayate*
3 Destroyer Division 30 – destroyers *Mutsuki, Kisaragi,* and *Yayoi*
4 Cruiser Division 18 – cruisers *Tatsuta* and *Tenryu*
5 Landing Force – *Patrol Boat 32* and *Patrol Boat 33* with 450 SNLF troops from 2nd Maizuru Special Landing Force

Offshore from Wake, Task Group 7.2, consisting of the SS *Tambor* and SS *Triton,* had been submerged throughout the day and was unaware of the events going on above them. The *Triton* noted plumes of smoke coming from Wake but thought little of it, and it was not until the two submarines surfaced after dark to recharge their batteries that they received news of the attack on Pearl Harbor, and of the day's events on Wake. Fearful of being mistaken for enemy craft, the two submarine commanders were advised to continue patrols around the atoll but to stay out of range of the 5in. coastal guns.

After dark, Cdr. Cunningham sent a dispatch to ComFourteen (Commandant 14th Naval District Pearl Harbor) reporting the day's attack: he had lost eight Wildcats, the 25,000-gallon Avgas tank had been destroyed (though ample Avgas remained), and 25 men had been killed and 30 injured, these being only the military casualties.

HERE THEY COME AGAIN!

December 9, day two of the siege of Wake, started with general quarters, sounded at 0500hrs, 45 minutes before dawn. Major Devereux set the atoll's defenses at Condition 1, having all phones manned and circuits checked. All weapons and fire-control instruments were fully manned, and battle lookouts were posted.

At 0545hrs the four serviceable Wildcats took off on their dawn patrol, reconnoitering 60–80 miles (100–130km) along the southern sector, the most likely route for Japanese bombers. The patrol returned at 0730hrs with nothing to report, and Maj. Devereux relaxed the defenses to Condition 2, with only half the guns manned and defense personnel rotated for work improving the defensive positions. Major Putnam consulted with Dan Teters to have two of the new aircraft shelters ramped below ground and roofed with "I" beams and timbers with a covering of coral sand. Tarpaulins were hung in the entrance, which allowed work to continue through the blackout at night, as well as offering more protection to the precious planes.

Orders to Cdr. Cunningham were that the NAS construction works were to continue, and so at a meeting with all his construction crews Dan Teters put his men back to work with the exception of the men he had sent to Maj. Devereux to assist the Marines.

As the morning wore on, many of the workers, civilian and military alike, kept as close as possible to shelters and foxholes, keeping one eye skyward looking for the expected bombers. At 1145hrs, almost on cue, 26 G3M bombers, again led by Lt. Cdr. Matsuda, came in at 13,000ft (3,960m). This time the

The USS *Triton.* Whilst patrolling south of Wake on December 10, the *Triton* fired four torpedoes at what was thought to be a Japanese ship. It was indeed part of Kajioka's invasion force. This was to be the first torpedo attack made by a US Pacific Fleet submarine in World War II. Had the *Triton,* along with the *Tambor,* been aware of the presence of the invasion fleet, they could well have assisted in repulsing the invasion along with VMF-211. (NARA)

bombers were spotted by the lookouts on top of the water tower at Camp 1, who informed the air–ground radio operator. He in turn relayed the information to the already-airborne midday combat air patrol. Two of the Wildcats dived onto tail-end stragglers of the bomber formation and succeeded in downing one of them before they had to disengage because of the increasing 3in. antiaircraft bursts coming up from Wake. Antiaircraft fire succeeded in damaging 12 of the 26 bombers, but all but the one shot down by the Wildcats managed to return to base.

Again, the bombers knew their targets, and bombs fell first on Battery A's 5in. guns, damaging the rangefinder, then around the 3in. guns of Battery E, damaging one of the four guns.

Next to receive the attention of the bombers was Camp 2: the civilian and Navy barracks, garages, a blacksmith shop, a storehouse, and machine shops were all destroyed. The NAS still under construction was also badly damaged, including the hangar and radio station, destroying a great proportion of Wake's radio gear. Worst hit of all at Camp 2 was the contractors' hospital building, which received direct hits and burst into flames. The hospital building, full of wounded from the previous day, burned to the ground, and it was only by the incredible efforts of Drs Shank and Kahn and the hospital staff that any of the wounded got out alive. Shank and Kahn then returned to the burning building to recover any medical instruments and supplies they could. A total of four Marines and 55 civilians died in the bombing.

The afternoon of December 9 saw what was to become all too familiar on Wake; the collection of dead and wounded, salvaging what could be reused among the ruins of tents and buildings, and the relocation of undamaged weapons and equipment. The regimental manner in which the Japanese bombers worked over Wake indicated to Maj. Devereux that the Japanese were working to a well-rehearsed pattern of bombing. The first day had seen the reduction of Wake's air defenses; today it had been buildings, stores, and antiaircraft positions, in particular Battery E's four 3in. guns. Devereux was convinced the Japanese had pinpointed Battery E's position, so he ordered Battery E to be moved overnight to a new position 600yds (550m) east and north, where the battery could still carry out its antiaircraft mission. Also, the damaged 3in. gun of Battery E was to be replaced by one from the unmanned Battery F on Wilkes.

The biggest problem remaining to Cdr. Cunningham was the loss of the contractors' hospital facilities. After reviewing the situation, he directed that two of the four reinforced concrete ammunition bunkers to the east of the airstrip were to be emptied and the ammunition stored in caches around the islands. this would make way for two 21-bed underground wards. The northern bunker, Bunker #13, was to be for Navy and CPNAB personnel under the direction of Dr Shank, and the southern bunker, Bunker #10, would be for the Marines under the direction of Dr Kahn. Splitting the two aid stations was intentional in order to have medical facilities and supplies as far

A formation of Japanese G3M bombers flies overhead. This is what the men defending Wake Island would have seen as they readied themselves for the daily bombing on the atoll. (Edward M. Young)

CAPTAIN HENRY "HAMMERING HANK" ELROD BAGS HIS SECOND JAPANESE BOMBER, DECEMBER 10, 1941 (pp. 44–45)

This scene depicts Captain Elrod in his F4F-3 Wildcat **(1)** diving, guns blazing, on a second G3M bomber of the Imperial Japanese Navy **(2)**, as his first "kill" spirals toward the ocean out of control and on fire **(3)**. The other G3M bombers scatter **(4)**. Wake Island can be seen to the north in the background **(5)**.

These two kills were credited to Capt. Elrod by Maj. Putnam, although Japanese after-action reports for that day state that only one G3M was lost over Wake. The Japanese command had estimated that three days of bombing would be sufficient to render Wake's defences reduced enough to enable a successful landing by the small invasion force, which had no close air support. The task of reducing Wake's defences was given over to the Chitose Kokutai of the 24th Air Flotilla under the command of Captain Ohashi Fujiro. On the first day of hostilities (December 8) 34 G3M bombers had caught the Wake defenders completely by surprise, destroying seven of the eight F4F Wildcats of VMF-211 on the ground (the eighth Wildcat was

damaged but repairable) and causing numerous casualties to pilots and ground-crew personnel. The Japanese bombers returned daily to bomb and strafe Wake's defences, but exaggerated claims by the Japanese air crews led Kajioka to believe that all aircraft and major defense installations had been destroyed; this was not the case, as Kajioka would find out for himself on the night of December 11.

Captain Elrod, nicknamed "Hammering Hank" by pilots and ground crew of VMF-211, was an aggressive, fearless combat pilot, distinguishing himself many times in air combat over Wake Island and also as an infantry officer defending "Hanna's Gun" on the December 23. He was mortally wounded whilst repulsing one of many assaults by SNLF troops during the bitter fighting around the airstrip. Elrod would receive the Medal of Honor (posthumously) for his gallantry on Wake, the first Marine officer to receive the award in World War II.

apart as possible. Having steel blast doors, the underground bunkers could be lit with the use of mobile generators, allowing 24-hour use. By nightfall both aid stations were up and running.

December 10 dawned with the expectation of a repeat of the day before. Defense and salvage operations were under way after a hasty breakfast. The expected bombers were a little earlier this time, 26 G3Ms in three waves approaching from the southeast, heading in over Peacock Point, intent on silencing the troublesome Battery E. Again, the Marine Wildcats rose to intercept the bombers, and this time Captain Elrod accounted for two bombers personally (although Japanese records show only one plane lost on December 10 to enemy fighters).

The bombers plastered the now vacated Battery E position, where dummy guns had been left to give the appearance that the battery was still there, while Battery E opened up on the bombers from its new position. Battery D on Peale received two passes from one of the flights, but suffered little damage and only one minor casualty. At least one bomber was seen to be on fire and smoking badly as the formation departed.

On Wilkes, which had previously been ignored by the bombers, similar attention was received to that of the other islands. Unluckily for the defenders, one stick of bombs fell on the contractors' cache of 125 tons of dynamite. Amazingly, only one Marine was killed, four were wounded, and one civilian was left suffering from shock.

Damage to the defense batteries was worse though. Batteries L and F's ammunition ready boxes were set off, and Battery L lost all accessories, light fittings, and anything else that wasn't bolted down. On inspection the gun crews found that all their fire-control instruments had been destroyed, save one gun telescope on Gun 2. The guns, though battered, would still fire.

Battery F had suffered similarly in the blast; one gun had suffered serious damage and was out of action, and that, along with the gun sent to replace the damaged gun with Battery E the day before, left Battery F with only two serviceable guns and with no gun crews.

Also severely damaged in the blast was one of the 60in. searchlights, which had been knocked over, resulting in major damage to arcs, bearings, and electronics. The attention given to the vacated position of Battery E confirmed Maj. Devereux's suspicions that the antiaircraft batteries were the bombers' prime targets and, fearful that Battery E's new position had been marked, he ordered the battery to be moved yet again, this time to the north of the airstrip in the interior angle of the lagoon. Once again, Battery E and the army of helpers toiled all night moving the guns and equipment, although this time the previously unmanned Gun 4 was dragged down to the south beach on Wake proper to serve as an antiboat gun. This gun would later feature heavily in the defense of Wake. Once again, by dawn Battery E was "manned and ready."

On the night of December 10, Captain Wilson of the Army Communication Unit requested permission from Maj. Devereux and Cdr. Cunningham to move his radio equipment to one of the two remaining reinforced concrete bunkers, to the east of the airstrip. Permission was given to use the second most southerly bunker, Bunker #11, and so during the night Capt. Wilson, with his men and a party of CPNAB assistants, dismantled the precious radio equipment, transported it to the bunker, and reinstalled it. Captain Wilson also put his radio at the disposal of the island commander; this was to be Cdr. Cunningham's only means of contact with Pearl Harbor throughout the siege. Cunningham would later move his command post into the bunker.

WE'RE HEADED FOR WAKE

Although the American public had already been warned by President Roosevelt to expect the worst from Wake Island, back in Pearl Harbor plans for a relief expedition to Wake were already being mooted at Admiral Kimmel's headquarters.

With the devastation of Pearl Harbor there could be little thought of any large-scale aggressive defense in the Pacific as envisaged in *Rainbow 5*, but the outlying island defense posts – such as Johnston, Palmyra, Midway, and Wake (Guam had already been written off) – if reinforced, could hold the Japanese advance sufficiently for the Pacific Fleet to recover enough to take to the offensive.

To reinforce these key defensive areas, all available Marine Corps forces were made ready. Admiral Kimmel had at his disposal two defense battalions (the 3rd and 4th), the remainder of the 1st Defense Battalion, and miscellaneous barracks and naval personnel. Pearl Harbor was already well stocked with equipment for these units, and the carrier USS *Saratoga* was en route from San Diego to Pearl Harbor with VMF-221 on her decks.

On December 10 (Pearl Harbor time) Admiral Kimmel's staff presented him with their plans to relieve Wake. Cruiser Division 6, comprising the heavy cruisers *Astoria*, *Minneapolis*, and *San Francisco*, would form the bulk of the force. The seaplane tender *Tangier* could be adapted into a troop transport to carry the troops and their equipment. To fuel the task force the fleet oiler *Neches* was available.

As a diversion a second task force, Task Force 11, of similar size to Task Force 14, less the transports and based around the carrier USS *Lexington*, would strike Japanese bases thought to exist on Jaluit, south of Wake. Both task forces would be supported by a third task force of similar size

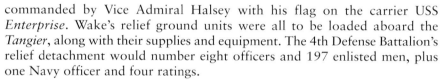

commanded by Vice Admiral Halsey with his flag on the carrier USS *Enterprise*. Wake's relief ground units were all to be loaded aboard the *Tangier*, along with their supplies and equipment. The 4th Defense Battalion's relief detachment would number eight officers and 197 enlisted men, plus one Navy officer and four ratings.

On board the *Tangier* the Marines loaded 200 tons of dry stores, two SCR-268 radars and one SCR-270-B radar, 12 .50-cal anti-aircraft machine guns, two height finders for 3in. antiaircraft guns, one m-4 director and one rangefinder for 5in. guns, as well as the spare parts requested in Cunningham's dispatches from Wake. Ammunition included 1,320 5in. powder charges, 1,200 rounds of 5in. service ammunition, 120 rounds of 5in. illuminating ammunition, 70 boxes of primers, 12,000 3in. antiaircraft shells (equipped with 30-second mechanical time fuses, not the virtually obsolete 21-second powder train variety that equipped Wake's batteries), 360,000 rounds of .50-cal armor-piercing bullets, 120,000 rounds of .50-cal tracer, 700,000 rounds of .30-cal ball, 69,000 rounds of .30-cal armor-piercing, 69,000 rounds of .30-cal tracer, and 480,000 .50-cal links.

The senior Marine officer with the relief force was originally to be 1st Lieutenant R. D. Heinl Jr., but he was replaced by Colonel H. S. Fassett when the decision was made to replace the naval commander with a Marine officer as island commander, it being rightly decided that Wake was no longer an NAS construction project but a military outpost. It was also intended that the relief force would evacuate all but essential civilian construction workers.

Loading complete, Admiral Fletcher awaited the arrival of the *Saratoga*, which arrived after dark at Pearl Harbor on 14 December. The *Saratoga* refueled during 15 December and, at 1600hrs, the *Tangier* and *Neches* with a temporary escort of four destroyers sortied out of Pearl Harbor to rendezvous out at sea with the *Saratoga* and the rest of Task Force 14. Help was finally on its way to the defenders of Wake; the Marines of the 4th Defense Battalion and VMF-221 were waved off by their Marine colleagues with a resounding "Give 'em hell!"

GUN 12

BATTERY L

GUN 11

GUN 10

2 SNLF

TAKANO

EVENTS

1 At 0300hrs the "100 picked men" of the 2nd Maizuru SNLF land on Wilkes Island's southern shore in two Daihatsu landing craft. Illuminated by Battery F's searchlight truck, they come under fire from .50-cal machine guns at positions 9 and 10. Japanese fire shoots out the searchlight and Takano and his men press inland toward Battery F's position.

2 With the Japanese closing in on Battery F, Capt. Platt orders the gun crews to withdraw to prepared positions to the east and west. At the same time, he orders Battery L's gun crews to move north and east to join Battery F's personnel. He and his command-post personnel move south to an assembly area located adjacent to machine-gun position 10.

3 Captain Platt orders two .30-cal machine guns moved from Kuku Point to join his position in order to provide flanking fire for his planned counterattack on the Japanese, who have taken up defensive positions in and around Battery F's gun position.

4 At dawn, Capt. Platt orders the attack to commence. He leads a mixed group of Marines and civilians from the west whilst a mixed group of Marines and civilians led by Lt. McAlister attacks from the east. A total of 30 Japanese troops take cover under and around Battery F's searchlight truck, who are all killed by .30-cal machine-gun fire from Corp. Johnson. The whole of Takano's force are killed, with the exception of two men who, wounded, are taken prisoner, with the Marines' corpsman treating their wounds.

FIGHTING ON WILKES ISLAND, DECEMBER 23, 1941

"100 picked men" of the SNLF land on Wilkes Island and attempt to push inland. Captain Platt organizes a successful defense and eventually the Japanese force is wiped out.

1DB

DEVEREUX

SUN 9

BATTERY F

US FORCES
1st Defense Battalion
A Headquarters, Wilkes strongpoint (Capt. Platt)
B Battery L, under the command of 2nd Lt. McAlister
C Two .30-cal machine guns under the command of Corp. Johnson
D Battery F, under the command of Gunner McKinstry

JAPANESE FORCES
2nd Maizuru SNLF
1 "100 picked men" under the command of Special Duty Ensign Takano

A 5in. gun, seen here in San Diego in October 1940, as Private Edward Eaton stands to provide a yardstick for the size of these guns. These weapons were the mainstay of the 1st Defense Battalion's armament. Six of these guns were in place on Wake in three two-gun batteries – Battery L on Kuku Point on Wilkes, Battery A on Peacock Point on Wake proper, and Battery B on Toki Point on Peale. (USMC)

THERE'S SOMETHING OUT THERE

Shortly before 0300hrs on December 11, Maj. Devereux sounded general quarters after receiving reports of ships sighted off the southern shores of Wake proper and Wilkes. Devereux then conferred with Maj. Putnam to see how many planes VMF-211 could put in the air, which was four. Devereux ordered Putnam to hold off from taking to the air until any firing took place in order to avoid the planes being spotted taking off and their number revealed to the Japanese.

Several hours earlier the *Triton*, whilst on the surface recharging her batteries, had spotted what looked like ships in the distance. She had submerged and leveled off at a depth of 120ft (37m), and, after tracking what appeared to be propellers at a low speed, loosed a salvo of four torpedoes from her stern tubes, the first torpedoes fired by a US submarine in World War II. The submarine crew heard a dull explosion, but no confirmation of a kill was possible. Later reports from the Japanese stated no damage to any of the invasion force by torpedoes.

Back on Wake, Maj. Devereux contacted Cdr. Cunningham informing him that the defense units had gone to general quarters and that four planes were readying for takeoff. Devereux also informed Cunningham that he had ordered all gun batteries to stay camouflaged and silent until ordered otherwise. In a postwar report by Cdr. Cunningham, he states that Devereux had requested permission to illuminate with searchlights and open fire much earlier, but that these requests were denied by Cunningham. This seems most unlikely as Devereux had far more knowledge and experience of his guns' capabilities, and rightly assumed that he was outgunned by the Japanese ships.

After-action reports by several other gun commanders also support Maj. Devereux's account. This disagreement between Devereux and Cunningham would become one of the main talking points in the Devereux–Cunningham controversy after the war.

Off Wake's southern shore, Rear Admiral Kajioka had arrived with his invasion force and had proceeded to take up positions for landing his troops. The bombardment squadrons took up their positions to commence bombarding the designated landing beaches, whilst the 450 SNLF troops attempted to boat into their armored steel-hulled Daihatsu landing craft. But the prevailing foul weather made boating the troops almost impossible, with men falling into the water around the troop ships and the landing craft being tossed about and in some cases overturned.

Whilst the boating fiasco continued, the bombardment squadrons began their run, paralleling the southern shores, led by Kajioka's flagship *Yubari*. By 0500hrs, as dawn was breaking over Wake, the *Yubari* reached a point 8,000yds (7.3km) south of Peacock Point and, turning westward, began her first run, followed by the other two cruisers *Tatsuta* and *Tenryu* and the rest of the bombardment squadron's ships, commencing fire on target areas along the southern shores at 0522hrs from Peacock point to Camp 1. Hits around Camp 1 set fire to diesel tanks, and only with prompt action from 2nd Lieutenant Poindexter in bringing the fires under control was further damage to the nearby generator and water-distillation equipment avoided.

Kajioka's ships received no return fire from the still-silent Wake, but the 5in. guns of Battery A on Peacock Point and Battery L on Kuku Point on Wilkes were already tracking the progress of their targets and twice had to be reminded of Maj. Devereux's order to hold their fire. By 0600hrs it was full daylight; Kajioka's ships had reversed their broadside run just west of Wilkes and, closing their distance offshore, had conducted a west-to-east run. Having reached Peacock Point, the *Yubari* again reversed course and closed her distance off Wake to 4,500–6,000yds (4.1–5.5km), now well within range of Battery A's 5in. guns.

At 0615hrs Devereux gave the command "open fire," and what happened next is given in the after-action report by Lieutenant Barninger, commanding officer of Battery A on Peacock Point:

At a range of forty-five hundred yards and a bearing of about 190° true we received the word to engage. We opened with an over and came down five hundred. At the opening salvo the cruiser turned and raced away from the battery on a zig-zag course, picking up speed rapidly. She now concentrated her fire on the battery position which had been disclosed by the initial firing… The fire from the cruiser continued to be over and then short throughout her firing. She straddled continually, but none of the salvos came into the position. They landed about 200–300 yards over then 100–200 yards short on the reef. The deflection was good.

The first salvo from our guns which hit her was fired at a range of 5,500–6,000 yards, bearing about 180 to 190. Both shells entered her port side about amidships just above the waterline. The ship immediately belched smoke and steam through the side and her speed diminished. At 7,000 yards two more hit

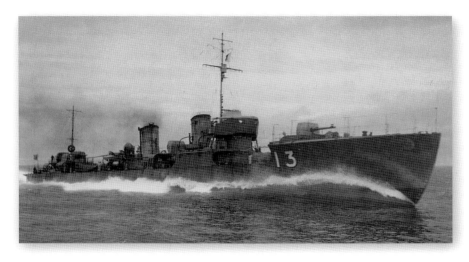

The IJN destroyer *Hayate*. This ship was fired upon by Battery L and subsequently exploded and sank with no survivors. It was the first Japanese surface craft to be sunk by US Naval forces in World War II. (Government of Japan)

BATTERY L SINKS THE *HAYATE*, EARLY DAWN, DECEMBER 11, 1941 (pp. 54–55)

The scene depicts a Battery L coastal-defense gun, under the command of Lt. McAlister, firing on the Japanese destroyer *Hayate*. Three successive hits caused the ship to explode and sink with all hands in two minutes. The gun crew in their sandbagged emplacements can be seen reloading the gun **(1)**, whilst the gun captain **(2)** checks their results through his field glasses, his communications operator at his side **(3)**. Local brush has been used to camouflage the gun emplacement. Other Japanese ships can be seen making a hasty retreat **(4)**.

The Japanese invasion force had been detected offshore of the south of Wake proper and Wilkes in the early hours of December 11. Realising, correctly, that his 5in. guns were outmatched by the Japanese cruisers' and destroyers' guns, Devereux gave orders that no guns were to be uncovered or open fire until he gave the order. Requests to illuminate the enemy ships with searchlights were also refused.

With dawn fully up and with a large proportion of the Japanese invasion fleet well within range of his 5in. guns, Devereux gave the order to open fire, with devastating results for the Japanese fleet; all three batteries on Wilkes, Wake proper, and Peale scored hits on cruisers, destroyers, and transports. This caused Kajioka to signal for the landing force to be recovered and the invasion force to retire back to base. As they did so, they were harassed by VMF-211's Wildcats, which resulted in more damage to ships, including the loss of the destroyer *Kisaragi* to "Hammering Hank" Elrod's bombs; it sank with the loss of all hands.

Rear Admiral Kajioka's invasion force had suffered badly from the Marine coastal guns (after the surrender of Wake the Japanese interrogated the Marine officers, wanting to know what had happened to the 8in. guns they had suffered from on the December 11 invasion attempt), with the loss of the *Hayate* and the *Kisaragi* as well as damage to the *Yubari* (Kajioka's flagship), *Oite*, *Tenryu*, *Tatsuta*, *Patrol Boat 33*, and the transport *Konga Maru*.

The invasion force limped back to base at Kwajalein, where, to his surprise, Kajioka was not relieved of his command but was instead given much more support in ships, ground-support aircraft (from the carriers *Hiryu* and *Soryu*), and landing-force troops.

The Japanese light cruiser *Yubari*, Rear Admiral Kajioka's flagship for both the first and second landing attempts on Wake. It lost the duel with Battery A on December 11, 1941. (USMC)

her in about the same place, but more probably slightly aft of the first two. Her whole side was now engulfed in smoke and steam and she turned to starboard again to try to hide in the smoke. At this time the destroyer which had accompanied the cruiser came in at high speed, tried to sweep between us to lay smoke, but a shell, an over, aft of the cruiser struck the forecastle of the destroyer. This hit was observed by Lt. Hanna, .50-caliber machine gun officer from his CP. The destroyer immediately turned, although fire was not directed at her, and fled. We continued to fire on the cruiser and although I am quite certain that we got two more into her side, I could not be sure of it. I am sure of the first four. The only hit I am certain of after this time was a hit on her forward turret. A shell hit the face of the turret and this turret did not fire again.

[...]

After we ceased firing, the whole fleet having fled and there being no other targets to engage, the cruiser lay broadside to the sea still pouring steam and smoke from her side. She had a definite port list. After some time she got slowly under way, going a short distance, stopping and continuing again; she was engulfed in smoke when she crept over the horizon.

Whilst Battery A was dueling with the *Yubari*, Battery L on Wilkes, commanded by Lieutenant McAlister, had opened fire on several ships within range with excellent effect. Although without a working rangefinder, it having been being blown out of operation in the dynamite explosion of December 10, Battery L was presented with a number of ships that virtually filled the battery's field of fire, consisting of the two transports *Kongo Maru* and *Kinryu Maru*, the two light cruisers *Tatsuta* and *Tenryu*, and three destroyers from Destroyer Division 29, the *Hayate*, *Oite*, and *Mochizuki*.

Having just executed a westerly turn from their run toward Wilkes' southern beach, the leading ship, the *Hayate*, came under fire from Battery L's guns, and, following the third salvo, was seen to explode, break in two, and sink. Within two minutes the *Hayate* and her 167 crew had disappeared beneath the waves with no survivors. The *Hayate* thus became the first Japanese surface craft to be sunk by US Naval forces in World War II. Cheers rose up from McAlister's gun crews momentarily, before being brought back to earth by a veteran NCO reminding them that there were still plenty of targets left! Gunfire was next turned on the *Oite*, which was so close to shore that Maj. Devereux had to deny requests from .30-cal machine-gun crews to open fire.

The 3in. antiaircraft gun located at the entrance to the airport building, December 2009. It is one of two remaining guns left on Wake Island. (Author's collection)

One hit was observed on the *Oite* before she was able to retire south under a smokescreen. The remaining ships of Cruiser Division 29, including the two transports, one of which sustained at least one hit, followed *Oite*'s lead and retired out of range. Battery L continued with harassing fire until the ships disappeared over the horizon. Battery L also registered hits on *Mockizuki* as she tried to retire out of range.

At the same time, Destroyer Division 30's ships came within range of Battery B under the command of Lieutenant Kessler at Toki Point on Peale. The two 5in. guns were engaging the destroyers *Yayoi*, *Mutsuki*, and *Kisaragi*, as well as the cruisers *Tenryu* and *Tatsuta*. Although Battery B received heavy return fire they sustained only two minor casualties. One of these was Lt. Kessler himself, wounded by a piece of shrapnel, and the other was Corporal Terry on Gun 2, when a recoil cylinder plug blew out, putting the gun out of action. Lieutenant Kessler's remaining 5in. gun scored at least one hit on the *Yayoi* before she too was out of range.

The whole invasion fleet retired south, heading back to Kwajalein, but Wake's Marines were not finished with them yet. At 0515hrs, well before dawn, Maj. Putnam with his three most senior and experienced pilots, Captains Elrod, Tharin, and Freuler, took off from Wake in three of the four serviceable Wildcats. The fourth Wildcat would not start but would join the other three in time for the air assault on the retreating Japanese task force. The four Wildcats rendezvoused north of Wake at 20,000ft (6,000m) and maintained that altitude until daybreak, when Putnam reconnoitered for any sign of enemy fighter aircraft supporting the task force.

As low cloud dispersed and the retiring ships of Kajioka's task force slipped beyond range of Wake's guns, VMF-211's four Wildcats pounced on the retiring ships, guns blazing. Elrod and Tharin singled out the destroyer *Kisaragi*, with one of Elrod's bombs landing aft and penetrating its deck. Trailing oil and smoke and ablaze, the *Kisaragi* slowed, limping off southwards.

Elrod had suffered damage from *Kisaragi*'s antiaircraft guns and so he headed back to Wake, and, although he made landfall, the resultant crash-landing rendered his aircraft good only for spares. The remaining three planes dived on the *Tenryu*, which sustained damage, as well as *Tatsuta*. They then returned to Wake to refuel and rearm, which they did a total of ten times before the Japanese ships were out of range.

Whilst these attacks were in progress, Maj. Putnam observed the limping *Kisaragi* "change from a ship to a ball of flame within a matter of seconds." The *Kisaragi* exploded (she was carrying an additional load of depth charges on her decks) and sank with the loss of her entire crew of 167 souls.

Putnam and Freuler, along with T/Sgt. Hamilton (who took over from Tharin) continued with assaults that caused damage and casualties on the transport *Kongo Maru*, but heavy antiaircraft fire had seriously damaged

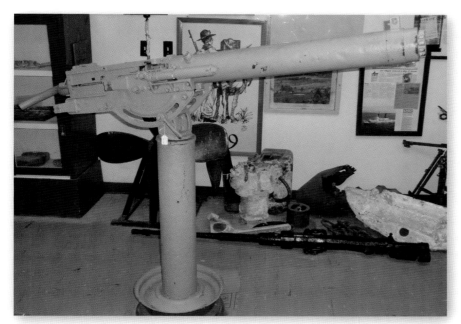

TOP
Water-cooled .50-cal antiaircraft machine gun. This is one of several machine guns uncovered on Wake over the years, located in the small museum within the airport terminal building. (Author's collection)

BOTTOM
Wake island airfield building. Built in the area of the original airstrip, inside is a small but excellent collection of artifacts dating from the battle and occupation of Wake. (Author's collection)

Capt. Freuler's aircraft. He managed to get it back to Wake in one piece, but VMF-211 was now down to only two planes.

However, the defenders of Wake would have little time to celebrate their victories, as 17 G3Ms in two waves came in at around 0915hrs. The last two serviceable Wildcats, piloted by Lt. Kinney and T/Sgt. Davidson, rose to meet the incoming bombers. Nine bombers commenced their bombing run on Peale's antiaircraft battery, to be met by heavy antiaircraft fire from 3in. and .50-cal guns on Peale. As they retired to the southwest they were pounced upon by T/Sgt. Davidson. The remaining eight bombers received the attention of Lt. Kinney, who flew straight into the formation in a head-on attack. As Kinney returned to base, the bombers heading home, he noted only seven bombers remained aloft, one of which was smoking badly.

The Japanese bombers suffered badly on the day's raid. In addition to Kinney's kill, Davidson accounted for a further two planes downed, and Battery D on Peale also observed at least three bombers smoking as they left, one reported to crash into the sea off Wilkes.

It could be argued that if the two submarines *Triton* and *Tambor* had been aware of the invasion force they could have joined in with VMF-211's harassing of the retreating *Kisaragi* and quite possibly sent a large proportion of the task force to the bottom of the ocean.

The three Japanese submarines, *RO-65*, *RO-66*, and *RO-67*, which had scouted ahead of the invasion force, took no part in the day's action, but one of them, probably *RO-66*, was spotted by Lieutenant Kliewer on his dusk patrol at around 1630hrs. Fully armed, Kliewer dived on the submarine, emptying his four .50-cal guns and dropping his two 100lb bombs at such a low altitude that bomb fragments holed both his wings and tail surfaces, before the submarine submerged. Kliewer returned to Wake and reported his actions to Maj. Putnam, who took off at dusk to reconnoiter the area, finding what appeared to be an oil slick in the area Kliewer had indicated. Upon his return he recorded that he was "almost certain" that Lt. Kliewer had sunk the enemy submarine.

Two other events took place on December 11. Major Devereux rightly observed that the Japanese bombers had pinpointed the location of Battery D on Peale, and so ordered the battery to be moved from Toki Point to the east end of Peale. With a mixed work party of Marines and civilians, Battery D moved guns and equipment through the night to its new location, although the sandbags were in such poor condition they had to be left behind. Because of a lack of replacements, empty cement bags and ammunition boxes had to be used for protection at the new gun position.

One final act took place. Commander Cunningham had earlier in the day ordered the mass burial of the dead still resting in the refrigerated reefer trailer at Camp 2, and so after darkness fell a CPNAB dragline excavator dug a trench, near to the southernmost bunker (the Marine aid station) and a burial party laid all Marine, Navy, and civilian dead alike in a common grave. Commander Cunningham, Maj. Devereux, and Dan Teters attended, as did a four-man firing party of Marines. No chaplain was present on Wake and so a CPNAB carpenter, who was also a lay preacher, John O'Neal, prayed for the souls of the departed. A bulldozer filled in the grave, which was then camouflaged. Orders were given that, in future, the dead would be buried where they fell in order to prevent the Japanese assessing casualties by counting grave crosses.

This photograph gives a good idea of what the pilots of VMF-211 might have seen as they attacked the formations of Japanese G3M bombers approaching Wake Island. (Getty)

WHEN TIME STOOD STILL

December 12 brought a new tactic from the Japanese. Shortly after 0500hrs, just 15 minutes after Battery D had reported in "guns manned and ready," the motors of two Kawanishi H6K Type 97 reconnaissance seaplanes were heard. Captains Freuler and Tharin took off to intercept them. One H6K dropped its bombs on the edge of the lagoon and bid a hasty retreat into the clouds with Captain Tharin in pursuit. Tharin dived at the lumbering seaplane and shot it down with no survivors. The other H6K unloaded its bombs near the airstrip, doing no damage, and raced back to base at Majuro.

For the rest of the day work continued on beach defenses and foxholes. On Wilkes, Battery L's battered 5in. guns received some much-needed maintenance. Lieutenant Kinney and his makeshift aviation maintenance crew performed yet another miracle by delivering one more serviceable Wildcat, put together from several others; this meant that VMF-211 now had three aircraft flying.

As noon drew close everyone worked near their foxholes, ready to dive in when the expected noon daily bombing arrived, but today there was none, much to the defenders' relief.

Another innovation came from Capt. Freuler, who succeeded in improvising a method of refueling the Wildcats' oxygen bottles from commercial oxygen bottles obtained from the construction workers' stores. This operation was so dangerous that Freuler insisted that he alone carried out the work.

Also on December 12, Cdr. Cunningham designated a commissary officer to take charge of distributing two hot meals per day from the contractors' mess at Camp 2, starting with the gun crews at the strongpoints. At 1100hrs on December 12 Washington, DC, time (0300hrs on December 13 at Wake), President Roosevelt held a press conference, and in response to a reporter's question of "How's Wake doing?" he replied: "So far as we know, Wake Island is holding out, has done a perfectly magnificent job. We are all very proud of that very small group of Marines who are holding the island. We have no further information today. They are holding out. We knew that very early this morning."

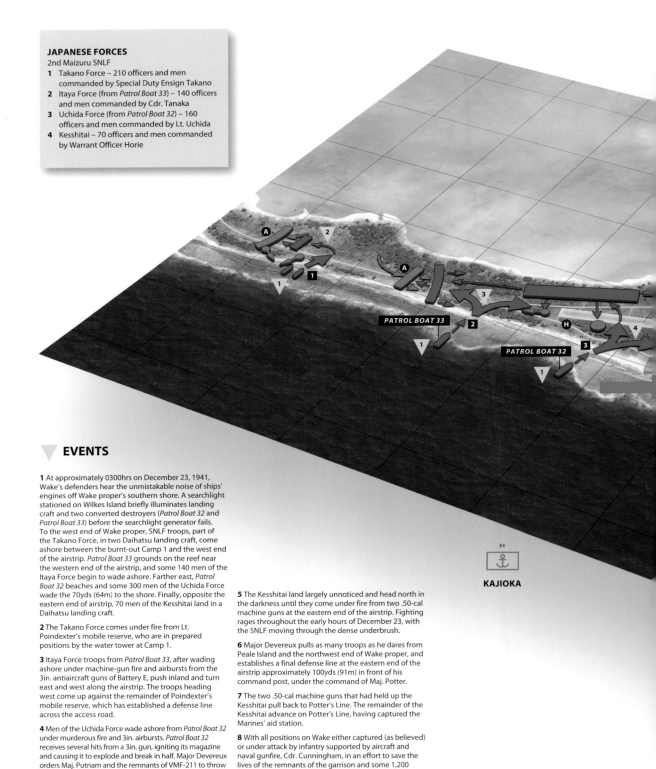

JAPANESE FORCES

2nd Maizuru SNLF

1 Takano Force – 210 officers and men commanded by Special Duty Ensign Takano
2 Itaya Force (from *Patrol Boat 33*) – 140 officers and men commanded by Cdr. Tanaka
3 Uchida Force (from *Patrol Boat 32*) – 160 officers and men commanded by Lt. Uchida
4 Kesshitai – 70 officers and men commanded by Warrant Officer Horie

KAJIOKA

▼ EVENTS

1 At approximately 0300hrs on December 23, 1941, Wake's defenders hear the unmistakable noise of ships' engines off Wake proper's southern shore. A searchlight stationed on Wilkes Island briefly illuminates landing craft and two converted destroyers (*Patrol Boat 32* and *Patrol Boat 33*) before the searchlight generator fails. To the west end of Wake proper, SNLF troops, part of the Takano Force, in two Daihatsu landing craft, come ashore between the burnt-out Camp 1 and the west end of the airstrip. *Patrol Boat 33* grounds on the reef near the western end of the airstrip, and some 140 men of the Itaya Force begin to wade ashore. Farther east, *Patrol Boat 32* beaches and some 300 men of the Uchida Force wade the 70yds (64m) to the shore. Finally, opposite the eastern end of airstrip, 70 men of the Kesshitai land in a Daihatsu landing craft.

2 The Takano Force comes under fire from Lt. Poindexter's mobile reserve, who are in prepared positions by the water tower at Camp 1.

3 Itaya Force troops from *Patrol Boat 33*, after wading ashore under machine-gun fire and airbursts from the 3in. antiaircraft guns of Battery E, push inland and turn east and west along the airstrip. The troops heading west come up against the remainder of Poindexter's mobile reserve, which has established a defense line across the access road.

4 Men of the Uchida Force wade ashore from *Patrol Boat 32* under murderous fire and 3in. airbursts. *Patrol Boat 32* receives several hits from a 3in. gun, igniting its magazine and causing it to explode and break in half. Major Devereux orders Maj. Putnam and the remnants of VMF-211 to throw up a defensive perimeter around Hanna's gun.

5 The Kesshitai land largely unnoticed and head north in the darkness until they come under fire from two .50-cal machine guns at the eastern end of the airstrip. Fighting rages throughout the early hours of December 23, with the SNLF moving through the dense underbrush.

6 Major Devereux pulls as many troops as he dares from Peale Island and the northwest end of Wake proper, and establishes a final defense line at the eastern end of the airstrip approximately 100yds (91m) in front of his command post, under the command of Maj. Potter.

7 The two .50-cal machine guns that had held up the Kesshitai pull back to Potter's Line. The remainder of the Kesshitai advance on Potter's Line, having captured the Marines' aid station.

8 With all positions on Wake either captured (as believed) or under attack by infantry supported by aircraft and naval gunfire, Cdr. Cunningham, in an effort to save the lives of the remnants of the garrison and some 1,200 civilians, gives the order to surrender the atoll.

JAPANESE LANDINGS, DECEMBER 23, 1941

Supported from the sea and air, Japanese troops land in force. After almost 12 hours of heavy fighting, US force

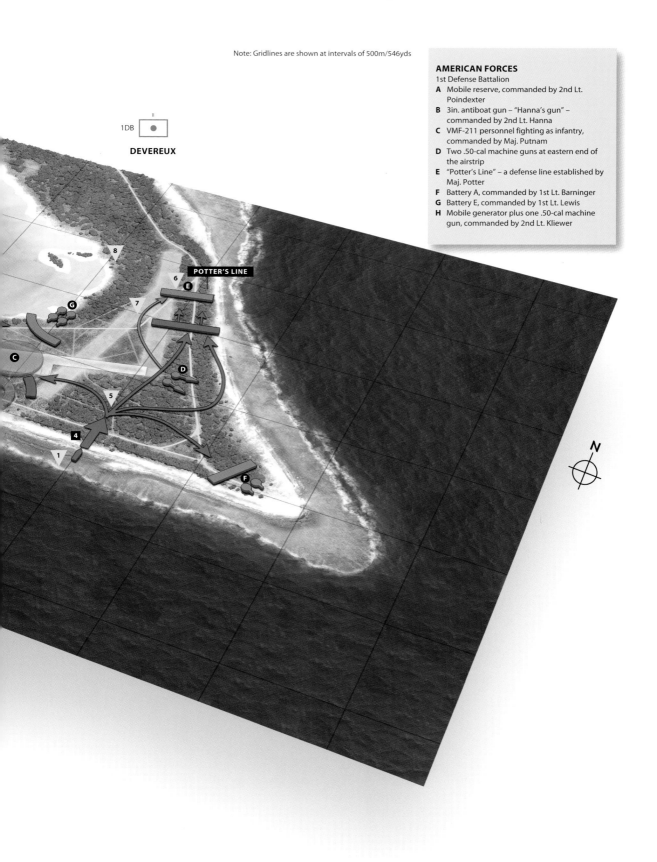

Note: Gridlines are shown at intervals of 500m/546yds

1DB ☐ ● ☐

DEVEREUX

POTTER'S LINE

AMERICAN FORCES

1st Defense Battalion

A Mobile reserve, commanded by 2nd Lt. Poindexter

B 3in. antiboat gun – "Hanna's gun" – commanded by 2nd Lt. Hanna

C VMF-211 personnel fighting as infantry, commanded by Maj. Putnam

D Two .50-cal machine guns at eastern end of the airstrip

E "Potter's Line" – a defense line established by Maj. Potter

F Battery A, commanded by 1st Lt. Barninger

G Battery E, commanded by 1st Lt. Lewis

H Mobile generator plus one .50-cal machine gun, commanded by 2nd Lt. Kliewer

An aerial shot of Wake Island, with an American SBD aircraft silhouetted in the foreground. After the Japanese capture of Wake, the US frequently harassed its occupiers with aerial attacks, and most photographic images of the atoll are from this period. (Official Navy Photograph)

With no mention of anyone other than Marines on Wake, President Roosevelt had inadvertently started the whole press fever over the "gallant Marines on Wake." At no time was any report received from the Marines on Wake; all reports, which continued right up until Wake surrendered, came from the island commander, Cdr. Cunningham, to CinCPAC (Commander-in-Chief, Pacific) at Pearl Harbor. The Japanese press reactions were less muted, stating: "The Imperial Navy shelled Wake Island and dealt heavy losses to military establishments – our side suffered some damage too."

At Wake, December 13 saw no Japanese bombers at all over the atoll, so the day was spent servicing weapons and distributing ammunition and food. Some took the opportunity to take a bath in the lagoon. But the day was not without incident for VMF-211. While taking off for the evening patrol, Capt. Freuler's plane swerved to the left without warning, headed straight for a large crane and a group of workers at the side of the runway. In an effort to avoid the crane Freuler swerved farther to the left, ditching his plane in the undergrowth, where it remained good only for spare parts. This left VMF-211 with only two airworthy Wildcats.

On December 14 the Japanese resumed their bombing, with three Kawanishi flying boats dropping their bombs around the airstrip at 0330hrs, causing no damage, and with the garrison not even returning fire. Just before noon, the 24th Air Flotilla resumed its bombing of Wake with 30 G3M bombers dropping bombs on Camp 1 and the lagoon, Peale and the west end of the airstrip being the target. Here bombs destroyed one of the last two serviceable Wildcats. With the aircraft ablaze, Lt. Kinney, along with T/Sgt. Hamilton and Aviation Machinist Mate James Hesson, sprinted to the plane and unbelievably rescued the still-serviceable motor from the burning wreck. Antiaircraft fire accounted for two of the bombers that day.

As the bombers retired to their base, Lt. Kinney and his crew installed the motor from the still-burning Wildcat F-10 into another plane they had been working on, F-9. By midnight, Kinney and his team had worked their magic once again and he was able to report to Maj. Putnam that VMF-211 had two planes airworthy.

December 15 saw no midday air raid on Wake, so work continued on defense works uninterrupted throughout the day. Major Putnam ordered Major Bayler and Captain Tharin to destroy VMF-211's classified documents, reserve ciphers, and codes. At 1730hrs a single Japanese aircraft was spotted well off to the east of Wake, and at 1800hrs, just after darkness fell, seven Kawanishi seaplanes from Majuro began their bombing run from 1,000ft (300m), dropping bombs on Camp 2 and bombing and strafing the area around Batteries D and B, but caused little damage with the exception of one civilian killed. Because of the low altitude, no return 3in. fire was possible.

December 16 saw the resumption of the Japanese midday raid from the south. At 1315hrs, 31 G3M bombers approached Wake from the east, at 18,000ft (5,500m), dropping their bombs on Peale and Camp 2. The two flying Wildcats were aloft and radioed altitude information to the gun crews on the ground before attacking the bombers. The Marine Wildcats scored no kills, the 3in. antiaircraft batteries downed one bomber and a further four left smoking heavily. The defenders received further harassment when at 1745hrs a single Kawanishi seaplane came in low and bombed Peale and Battery D, but caused little damage.

Shortly after midnight, lookouts on Wilkes reported sighting ships, approximately 12 in number, offshore to the south. The defenders went to general quarters, but with no further sightings the defenders were stood down shortly before dawn.

At 0600hrs on December 17, Lt. Kinney proudly reported to Maj. Putnam that he now had four Wildcats airworthy. Putnam would later state:

> These three, Lieutenant Kinney, Technical Sergeant Hamilton and Aviation Machinist's Mate Hesson, with the assistance of volunteers among the civilian workmen, did a truly remarkable and almost magical job. With almost no tools and a complete lack of normal equipment, they performed all types of repair and replacement work. They changed engines and propellers from one airplane to another, and even completely built up new engines and propellers from scrap parts salvaged from wrecks. They replaced minor parts and assemblies, and repaired damage to fuselages and wings and landing gear; all this in spite of the fact that they were working with new types with which they had had no previous experience and were without instruction manuals of any kind. In the opinion of the squadron commander their performance was the outstanding event of the whole campaign.

But Kinney's four planes became three when one was written off during takeoff in the afternoon. At 1317hrs some 27 G3Ms from Roi came in over Wake at 19,000ft (5,800m), this time concentrating on Wilkes' defenses and what remained of Camp 1. They succeeded in razing the defense battalion's tents to the ground, including the mess hall and quartermaster storage, as well as one of the freshwater evaporators. Antiaircraft fire brought down one of the bombers.

Wreckage of the F4F-3 piloted by Capt. Freuler, who, following aerial combat on December 22, destroyed two Japanese dive-bombers, including the one carrying Petty Officer 1st Class Kanai Naburo, the man credited with dropping the fatal bomb on the USS *Arizona*. (NARA)

65

In addition to the midday bombing, at 1750hrs eight Kawanishi seaplanes hit Wake, bombing and strafing the whole area but achieving little in the way of damage. Also on December 17, Cdr. Cunningham received a communiqué from Pearl Harbor requesting a progress report on the NAS construction works and asking for specific dates for when certain works would be complete. It was obvious that Pearl Harbor thought construction works on Wake were continuing despite all the reports of damage and casualties Cunningham had been making since the first raid on December 8.

Having calmed down sufficiently to pen a reply, Cdr. Cunningham commenced with a preface of the day's air raids and damage report. He then continued with a matériel report, stating that half of his trucks and emergency equipment was destroyed, the best part of his diesel oil and commercial explosives was gone, and that the Navy garage, blacksmiths, machine shops, and warehouses no longer existed. Cunningham stated that his main priority was defending Wake and keeping the garrison alive at the present time, also pointing out that no nighttime work was possible because of blackout conditions and that daytime work suffered from the lack of radar and early warning for the daily bombings. Furthermore, the morale of the civilian contractors was "generally bad," not surprisingly.

Cunningham closed his report stating that no deadlines or completion dates could be given at this time unless enemy pressure could be lifted. Wake would receive no further requests for progress reports from Pearl Harbor.

December 18 was a quiet day, with only a lone Japanese plane overhead at 25,000ft (7,620m), out of range of the antiaircraft guns. This was probably a photoreconnaissance plane from Roi.

December 19 dawned with most of the defensive works now as complete as they could be, including two partially underground and covered revetments at the airstrip, which allowed Lt. Kinney to work round the clock on his three remaining Wildcats.

At 1050hrs 27 G3M bombers approached Wake at 18,000ft (5,500m), again to be met by two Wildcats, the third being worked on in the underground revetment. Targets for the bombers today were the airstrip, Camp 1, and what was left of the PanAm facilities, which were by now deserted. Batteries D and E opened up on the bombers, hitting four, one of which was seen to crash into the sea.

December 20 dawned gloomy with heavy rain and poor visibility, which probably dissuaded the Japanese from their daily bombing run out of Roi, giving Wake's defenders a welcome quiet day free from bombing.

At 1530hrs, much to the amazement of Wake's defenders, though not to Cdr. Cunningham, who was expecting it, a Navy PBY flying boat landed in the lagoon. Its pilot was carrying detailed information for Cdr. Cunningham on the relief expedition heading for Wake. Cunningham's orders told him to prepare to evacuate all but essential civilian personnel. A loading plan of the transport *Tangier* was included, detailing troops and equipment aboard to reinforce the garrison. Cunningham was further advised of fighter aircraft reinforcements, VMF-211, good news indeed for Wake.

After delivering the orders to Commander Cunningham, the two PBY pilots enquired of the location of the hotel so that they could freshen up and have a meal; one Marine showed them the burnt-out remains of the Pan Air Hotel, and told him: "Welcome to Wake!"

All through the night all hands penned letters to mothers, wives, and girlfriends, as the PBY pilots had agreed to take these letters out with them

the next day. Commander Cunningham, Maj. Devereux, Maj. Putnam, and Cdr. Greey compiled reports to be taken back to Pearl Harbor by Major Bayler who, his work on Wake now complete, still had orders to return to Pearl Harbor "by first available government air transportation."

The ill-fated Bureau of the Budget official, Mr Hevenor, who had missed the departure of the Philippine Clipper on December 8, was to leave on the PBY as well until it was pointed out that Navy regulations required a Mae West life jacket and a parachute for all aboard a Navy aircraft, and as none was available Hevenor would have to stay. Mr Hevenor eventually left Wake courtesy of the Japanese Navy, en route to a POW camp in China.

At 0700hrs on December 21 the PBY with all its mail and Maj. Bayler aboard gunned its engines and lifted off from the lagoon, headed for Pearl Harbor. News of the relief expedition was filtering through the island when out of the blue a far more ominous sign arrived over Wake from the Japanese. At 0850hrs 29 Aichi D3A1 Type 99 bombers covered by 18 Mitsubishi A6M2 Type 00 fighters from the carriers *Hiryu* and *Soryu*, which had been detailed to Wake on their return from the attack on Pearl Harbor, pounced on Wake's defenders, signaling that the Japanese had won the race to reach Wake. With carrier aircraft in the area, an invasion fleet would not be far away. The dive-bombers bombed and strafed the whole atoll, and at such a low altitude 3in. antiaircraft fire was ineffective, though .50-cal machine-gun fire did hit at least three aircraft. The last two Wildcats, one of which would not start up, did not even have time to take to the air. As soon as the Japanese planes left, heading back to their carriers, Maj. Putnam climbed into the only serviceable Wildcat and headed off after the Japanese, hoping to locate their carriers, but his attempt was unsuccessful.

Within three hours of the carrier planes departing at 1220hrs, 33 G3M bombers out of Roi arrived over Wake, plastering Peale and Camp 2 in two formations, seeking out Battery D, which was hit directly when a bomb fell squarely inside the gun-director emplacement, killing Sergeant Wright and wounding the range officer and three enlisted men.

One of two sole surviving 3in. guns from the battle of Wake Island. This one is located amongst the accommodation buildings on the site of what was Camp 2. (Author's collection)

The day's damage left Maj. Devereux with a dilemma. The only remaining director for the 3in. antiaircraft guns belonged to Battery E on Wake proper, but Battery E had no height finder, whilst Battery D did have. After considering the options, Devereux instructed Battery D's height finder moved, along with equipment and a single gun, to Battery E, which would now be a fully manned, fully equipped battery for the first time. Devereux further ordered two of Battery D's guns moved to a new location on Peale to act as beach-defense guns, and the one remaining gun to stay at Battery D's old location amid dummies to create the impression that the battery was still intact. Devereux also ordered Battery F on Wilkes to open fire during any air raids, in order to give the impression that the battery was still intact and working even though it had only two guns. This meant that all Devereux had for effective aerial defense of Wake was four 3in. antiaircraft guns (Battery E), a number of .50-cal antiaircraft machine guns, and two Wildcat fighters (one of which took an age to start up).

A credit to the civilian volunteers who manned Battery D's guns throughout came from the strongpoint commander Captain Godbold, who said: "The civilians who served with this battery were of inestimable value – under the capable leadership of Sgt. Bowsher they soon were firing their gun in a manner comparable to the Marine manned guns. Before the surrender of the island some of these men were slated to be evacuated, however the entire gun crew offered to stay on the island and serve with the battery."

On the morning of December 22, two Wildcats were in commission, although one still suffered starter trouble, which delayed Capt. Freuler taking off on the mid-morning patrol along with Lt. Davidson. Davidson had been patrolling the northern approaches to Wake for the past hour at 12,000ft (3,650m) when he spotted incoming enemy planes. Captain Freuler, who was patrolling to the south, then turned and headed north to join Davidson. The incoming Japanese planes were 33 Type 97 bombers escorted by six A6M2 fighters, all from the *Hiryu* and *Soryu* carriers. Without hesitation, Capt. Freuler dived into the formation of dive-bombers, guns blazing. Freuler saw the formation scatter, with one of the dive-bombers trailing smoke as it headed down to the sea. Freuler turned and dived onto a second Type 97, which exploded only 50ft below him, sending flames and debris about the Wildcat. Freuler's plane was badly scorched and, with manifold pressure dropping and his controls reacting sluggishly, Freuler headed back. He saw

Wreckage of F4F-3s from VMF-211 on Wake. This photograph was taken by the Japanese after the fall of Wake. In the foreground is plane 211-F-11, flown by Captain Elrod on December 11, when he successfully bombed and sank the Japanese destroyer *Kisaragi*. (NARA)

Lt. Davidson doing battle with the six A6 fighters, one of which broke off and came astern of Freuler, guns blazing. Bullets penetrated the fuselage and bulkhead of Freuler's plane, wounding him in the back and shoulder. Freuler, with no other option, put his plane into a steep dive to try and make his adversary think he was going to crash into the sea. This worked, and the Japanese fighter broke off his attack and returned to attack Lt. Davidson. Freuler pulled out of the dive and managed to get his plane back to the airstrip, but a crash-landing finally finished the Wildcat's flying career. Freuler last saw Lt. Davidson on the tail on one Japanese fighter, with another on his. The fighter that had attacked Freuler, on returning to the pack, attacked Davidson. Davidson was never seen again, and the pilot of the A6M2 fighter, Petty Officer Third Class Isao Tahara, was credited with both kills. It was later learned that the second dive-bomber Capt. Freuler had shot down, and which had exploded beneath him, killing all three crew members, had on board as bomb aimer Petty Officer First Class Naburo Kanai, the man credited with dropping the fateful bomb that penetrated the deck of the USS *Arizona*, the one that caused the massive explosion which sent the battleship to the bottom of Pearl Harbor. The ship had now been avenged somewhat.

Conditions for the men en route to Wake Island would have been similar to those in this photograph of Air Force personnel shown in their berths in a troop ship. (NARA)

With no planes left to defend the skies above Wake, the dive-bombers were at liberty to drop their bombs with only .50-cal machine guns to disrupt them, though the Marines considered their bombing to be poor and inaccurate, and it caused little damage and no casualties.

In the afternoon, knowing that an invasion force must be imminent, ground defenses were intensified. On Peale the beach defenses around the two 3in. guns were completed. On Wilkes, Captain Platt issued orders to Battery F's 3in.-gun commander, Gunner McKinstry, that in the event of a landing he was to fire on the boats as long as his guns could be depressed to hit them, and then to fall back and join Battery L's Marines as infantry.

On Wake proper, with no planes left, Maj. Putnam reported with the remnants of VMF-211, less than 20 officers and men, to Maj. Devereux, to be deployed as the defense commander saw fit. Devereux had Putnam and his men remain at the airstrip ready to support the lone 3in. antiaircraft gun that had been deployed as beach defense. The indomitable Lt. Kinney was sent to the hospital suffering from complete exhaustion and severe diarrhea. As one Wake officer put it: "All that can be done is being done, but there is so little to do it with."

WE'LL BE THERE FOR CHRISTMAS

Whilst events were unfolding on Wake, the relief expedition, Task Force 14, was under way from Pearl Harbor. On December 15 (Pearl Harbor time) the *Tangier* and *Neches*, along with their temporary escort of four destroyers, had sortied out of Pearl Harbor after dusk, while the *Saratoga*, with VMF-221 aboard, fueled up for the trip to Wake. Departing Pearl Harbor in two groups, the *Tangier* and *Neches* and escort would leave first, to be joined by the *Saratoga* later at sea. Also aboard the *Saratoga* was Major Verne J. McCavl, who was to replace Cdr. Cunningham as island commander.

At 1115hrs on December 16 (Pearl Harbor time), after some delays, the *Saratoga* and her escort of three heavy cruisers and nine destroyers slipped out of Pearl Harbor. They expected to reach Wake by December 23 (December 24 on Wake). Refueling was to be at the discretion of the task-force commander, Rear Admiral Frank Jack Fletcher USN. The timing of the refueling of the task force was to prove fatal for Wake.

The speed of the task force was painfully slow, as it could go only as fast as the slowest ship, which was the *Neches* at 12 knots. On board the *Tangier* the Marines prepared themselves for battle, the technicians trying to familiarize themselves with the mysterious new-fangled radar sets stowed aft. Battle sights for the 3in. guns of the defense battalion were manufactured aboard ship to turn the guns into dual-purpose antiaircraft/antiboat guns, and a system was devised to allow the .50-cal machine guns to be offloaded onto shore barges in the ready position, to ward off enemy air attack.

This photograph of a .30-cal machine gun shows the kind of defense position the Marines on Wake Island would have established as they attempted to drive the Japanese back. (NARA)

The USS *Saratoga*, the carrier of Task Force 14, carrying VMF-221 reinforcements for Wake and part of the task force recalled by Vice Admiral Pye on December 23, 1941. The pilots of VMF-221, on receiving the word that the task force was being recalled, begged for permission to take off and head for the atoll. (NARA)

At 1500hrs on December 17 (Pearl Harbor time) Admiral Kimmel, in accordance with orders from President Roosevelt and Secretary of the Navy, turned over temporary command of the Pacific Fleet (including Task Forces 8, 11, and 14) to Vice Admiral Pye, who would take command until the arrival of Kimmel's permanent replacement, Admiral Chester W. Nimitz, which would be in late December. Admiral Kimmel was to be the "sacrificial lamb" for the Navy and the Pearl Harbor debacle. Although not enthusiastic about the task force on its way to Wake, Vice Admiral Pye allowed it to continue for the moment, but he was in no mood to lose any more ships whilst he commanded the Pacific Fleet. On December 18, Pye ordered Task Group 7.2, the Wake submarine patrol, to withdraw in order to avoid being taken as enemy ships by the approaching task force.

With the news of a heavy concentration of aviation strength in the Marshalls and the news from Wake of carrier-based planes overhead, Task Force 11, with the USS *Lexington*, was diverted from diversionary attacks on the Marshalls to support Task Force 14's approach to Wake.

By 0800hrs on December 22 (Wake time), Task Force 14 was only 515 miles (830km) from Wake. Rear Admiral Fletcher was in receipt of all communications from Wake and, fearing that he may have a fight on his hands when he arrived at Wake, ordered his fighting ships to refuel for fear of running out in the middle of a battle. And so, by 0800hrs on December 23 (Wake time), Task Force 14 was still 425 miles (685km) from the atoll. This was as close as they would get.

Back at Pearl Harbor, during the night of December 21–22 (December 22–23 at Wake), Vice Admiral Pye conferred with his staff on what to do with Task Force 14. It was decided to launch VMF-221 from the *Saratoga* to Wake and then for the *Saratoga* to retire to Pearl Harbor. At the same time, the *Tangier* was to strike out for Wake on her own, with the Marine detachment aboard. This would almost certainly have resulted in the destruction of *Tangier* and the Marines on board.

Before Admiral Fletcher could carry out these orders, he received fresh orders countermanding the previous ones. After making his first decision, Pye had met with Secretary of the Navy Knox, who, after surveying the damage at Pearl Harbor, had commented to Pye that "Wake is a liability, not an asset."

At 0811hrs on December 22 (Pearl Harbor time) some 2½ hours before Wake surrendered, Task Force 14 was recalled. On board Fletcher's flagship *Astoria* and on the *Saratoga* and *Tangier* reaction to the order ranged from shame to anger. On the *Astoria*, Fletcher's staff officers begged him to ignore the order and press on to Wake. Fletcher eventually left the bridge so that he could not officially hear this "mutinous talk." On the *Saratoga*, VMF-221 pilots pleaded to be allowed to fly to Wake but were refused. On the *Tangier*, only the intervention of senior Marine officers prevented the ship from being taken over by the Marines on board. None on board Task Force 14 would ever forgive Pye for abandoning Wake to its fate.

ENEMY ON THE ISLAND, ISSUE IN DOUBT

The night of December 22–23 on Wake was marred by rain squalls and rough seas. Rear Admiral Kajioka had set sail from Roi on the morning of December 21 with his much-reinforced Wake occupation force. This time, Kajioka had at his disposal four heavy cruisers, two old light cruisers, six destroyers, one auxiliary seaplane tender, two patrol boats, and three medium transports, as well as three submarines scouting ahead of the task force and the carrier task force already operating to the north of Wake. One of the main tasks for the submarine scouting force was to confirm or deny the presence of motor torpedo boats at Wake, of great concern to Kajioka. Kajioka received word on December 22 that no boats had been sighted. Kajioka's landing force had been greatly increased; he had over 1,000 SNLF troops and additionally some 1,500 bluejacket landing-party troops at his disposal, as well as ground-support aircraft from the *Soryu* and *Hiryu*.

At around 0200hrs on December 23, Kajioka commanded the invasion to begin. Earlier, at around 0100hrs, Marine lookouts on Peale had seen "vivid irregular flashes" in the sky north of Peale; this was in fact the Japanese cruisers *Tenryu* and *Tatsuta*, tasked with a diversionary bombardment of Peale. They had, because of the bad weather and high seas, wandered past Peale to the north and bombarded nothing but open sea. The garrison was now alert to the presence of the invasion force.

Moreover, at 0145hrs, word came to Maj. Devereux in his new command post in the last remaining unoccupied bunker to the east of the airstrip (Devereux had moved in on December 14) that the enemy was landing on Toki Point on Peale. Major Devereux ordered 1st Lieutenant Kessler, commanding officer of Battery B at Toki Point, to investigate and report back. At the same time, Devereux placed all units on alert. Kessler reported back to Devereux that no landings were in progress, although boats were "believed to be somewhere offshore." Lieutenant Poindexter, in command of the mobile reserve of eight Marines with four .30-cal machine guns, along with a few Marine admin and supply personnel as well as 15 Navy ratings under the command of Boatswain's Mate 1st Class James Barnes, all with only one truck for transportation, on hearing the reports of landings at Toki Point requested permission from Maj. Devereux to move out from his position at Camp 1 to Toki Point. This Devereux gave, but on receiving word from Lt. Kessler that no landings were in progress, had Poindexter with his truckload of men intercepted and held at Devereux's command post.

At 0215hrs it was evident that a landing attempt was in progress. Lights were observed not only off Peale to the north but also to the south off both Wake proper and Wilkes. At 0230hrs reports from Peacock Point of "barge-like shapes" offshore were received at Devereux's command post. These were in fact the two patrol boats heading for the southern shore of Wake proper. Major Devereux, along with his executive officer Major Potter and two switchboard operators, tried to keep up with the deluge of reports coming in on the telephone line, whilst at the same time keeping Cdr. Cunningham informed of developments. Major Devereux ordered Lt. Poindexter to set up a defense line between the end of the airstrip and Camp 1.

At 0235hrs reports from Wilkes of landing craft engines being heard prompted Captain Platt to request to illuminate them with one of his 60in. searchlights. Permission given, the searchlight lit up not only Wilkes' southern beaches but Wake proper's as well, where *Patrol Boat 32* and *Patrol Boat 33*

as well as landing craft were fast approaching the beaches. Neither of the 5in. batteries on Peacock Point and Kuku Point could register the approaching craft, leaving only .50- and .30-cal machine guns to resist a landing. The only gun in the area that could fire on the landing craft was the 3in. antiaircraft gun that Devereux had placed on the southern beach by the airstrip parking area, but it was unmanned. Lieutenant Robert Hanna, in charge of the airstrip's antiaircraft machine guns, quickly recognized the situation and, with a scratch gun crew of one Marine (Corporal Ralph Holewinski) and three civilians, set out at the double for the lone 3in. gun. Major Devereux, appreciating the critical importance of the gun and of holding the position, ordered Maj. Putnam to take the remnants of his VMF-211 men to support Hanna and defend the gun position.

With the whole atoll at general quarters, Lt. Poindexter's mobile reserve with four .30-cal machine guns was at the west end of the airstrip, facing east and firing on SNLF troops already ashore from *Patrol Boat 32* and *Patrol Boat 33*. At Camp 1 four .30-cal machine guns and a defense line was set up north and south of the access road, facing east. Lieutenant Hanna and his scratch crew covered by Maj. Putnam and his men were south of the airstrip, with Hanna's gun firing on *Patrol Boat 32* and *Patrol Boat 33*.

In the way of any attempt to move west from *Patrol Boat 32* and *Patrol Boat 33* was Lt. Kliewer, with three aviation Marines, dug in and manning the generator powering the electric detonators for the mines along the airstrip, ready to detonate them at a moment's notice. Just northwest of Kliewer's foxhole were two .50-cal machine guns posted to cover the airstrip; a similar two machine guns were at the eastern end of the airstrip.

Shortly before 0300hrs, Maj. Devereux lost wire communication with Camp 1, Maj. Putnam and VMF-211, Lt. Hanna's command post, and Battery A, as well as tactical-line communication with Capt. Platt on Wilkes, although he could still at this time be reached on the telephone line. It is most probable that these communication cables, all laid above ground, were discovered by the SNLF troops and cut. Devereux still had a radio-communication network, but this had never worked well and on December 23 did not work at all. With no communication personnel spare at his command post to troubleshoot the broken wires, Maj. Devereux was practically in the dark as to what was happening where – this would prove to be a major factor in Devereux's conduct of the defense. On reaching the 3in. gun on the beach, Hanna and his crew fumbled in the dark for ammunition; having found it, Holewinski and the three civilian volunteers

LEFT
A Sperry 60in. searchlight. Three of these truck-mounted searchlights were in place on Wake, albeit briefly, the Japanese landings on December 23, 1941. (USMC)

RIGHT
The Browning M1917 .30-cal machine gun was also a mainstay of the defensive weapons used on Wake, shown here in Burma in 1944. First used in World War I, it would prove highly effective throughout World War II and even into the Korean War. (NARA)

MAIZURU LANDING FORCE SUFFERS HEAVY CASUALTIES FROM HANNA'S GUN, DECEMBER 23, 1941 (pp. 74–75)

The scene depicts the beached *Patrol Boat 32* **(1)** on the reef off the southern shore of Wake proper, under heavy 3in. artillery fire and ablaze. It would eventually explode and break in half. Men of the SNLF and landing-force sailors are clambering down Jacob's ladders and ropes from the burning vessel into waist-deep surf **(2)**, rifles held above their heads, and illuminated by the fire. Many of them wear white sashes tied across their chests and white bands tied to their helmets to aid recognition in the dark. They suffered over 100 casualties on the beach and in the surf from 3in. airbursts **(3)** and machine-gun and small-arms fire. The officers and NCOs urge their troops on **(4)**, some with Japanese flags tied to their bayonets on the end of their rifles **(5)**.

These flags were intended to be used to mark the Japanese positions for aerial recognition by fighters and dive bombers from the *Hiryu* and *Soryu* come daylight. The positioning of these flags, particularly on Wilkes, where they had been placed around the captured Battery F gun position and reported to Maj. Devereux, led him to believe, along with the loss of radio and telephone communication with his troops on Wilkes, that Wilkes had been captured by the Japanese landing force. This situation was totally incorrect, and the Wilkes defenders had in fact eliminated all the Japanese landing-force troops by dawn on December 23, but the defenders were not able to contact Maj. Devereux to inform him that Wilkes was secure before Cdr. Cunningham gave the order to Devereux to surrender.

The Japanese SNLF troops were the Imperial Japanese Navy's elite troops, equivalent to the US Marines. They were well armed and equipped and well trained, preferring to use the sword and bayonet in preference to the rifle or machine gun when on the offensive. However, they were well versed in the use of artillery and machine guns when on the defensive, as the US Marines would discover in the future.

loaded while Hanna sighted the gun by "Kentucky methods" (looking down the barrel) on the nearest target, *Patrol Boat 32*. Being around only 500yds (457m) away, the target was hard to miss. His first shell hit the bridge superstructure, wounding the captain and navigator and killing three crew. With SNLF troops from the Uchida and Itaya companies swarming down ropes and Jacob's ladders from the patrol boats, Hanna put 14 more 3in. high-velocity rounds into *Patrol Boat 32* before it exploded and burst into flames, illuminating the whole area.

With both boats under fire, the crews joined the SNLF troops on the beach and pushed inland. As Uchida's units pushed eastwards in an effort to silence the troublesome 3in. gun of Lt. Hanna, they ran into Maj. Putnam's defense line around Hanna's guns. Despite attempts to outflank him, Putnam's perimeter held, but was pushed back until his men were almost surrounded.

With the landings obviously concentrated on the southern beaches, Maj. Devereux sent word to Captain Godbold at Battery D on Peale to send one gun section (nine men) by truck to Devereux's command bunker for further deployment as infantry. This Godbold did, the section arriving some 15 minutes later. Major Devereux's orders to the section, under the command of Corp. Graves, was to continue south past the airstrip and then work west toward Lt. Hanna and Maj. Putnam.

Meanwhile, light from the burning patrol craft revealed to Lt. Poindexter that some men of the Uchida force were working their way across the southern shore road toward the airstrip. Poindexter directed one of his .30-cal machine-gun sections to fire on the enemy, who had disappeared in the darkness into the brush. At the same time, Poindexter heard machine-gun fire coming from the area of Camp 1, where his remaining four .30-cal machine guns were manned by a mixture of Marines and bluejackets. Leaving Gunnery Sergeant Wade to carry on with the firefight, Poindexter returned to Camp 1 to find that

The southern shore of Wake proper. This area is where *Patrol Boat 32* and *Patrol Boat 33* beached on the reef, which can be seen just beyond the breakers in this photograph. The last remaining pieces of the two patrol boats were lost in the last typhoon. The deafening noise from the breakers on the coral reef is still much in evidence today. (Author's collection)

all four machine guns were firing on two landing craft attempting to cross the reef and land east of Wilkes' channel entrance. The .30-cal bullets were making no impression on the armored landing craft, which were again attempting to breach the reef. Taking advantage of the stalemate, Lt. Poindexter formed two teams of grenadiers to move down to the water's edge and bombard the landing craft with grenades. One team consisted of Poindexter and Boatswain's Mate James Barnes, whilst the other team was made up of Mess Sergeant Gerald Carr and a civilian, R. R. Rutledge, who had served as an officer in the US Army during World War I in France. Boatswain's Mate Barnes and Rutledge scored hits on the landing craft, inflicting casualties, but the boats broke through the reef and were able to land troops, who moved inland into the brush and headed east and north toward Camp 1. As they advanced, the SNLF troops found and cut the overground communication wires connecting to Devereux's command bunker. Devereux heard no more from Poindexter and the mobile reserve other than from a panicky civilian who had worked his way from Camp 1 to Devereux's command post, telling of Camp 1 being overrun by the Japanese, the men of the mobile reserve being bayoneted and slaughtered to a man.

On Peale, Capt. Godbold had sent out patrols eastwards from Toki Point along the beach and lagoon shores to check for any signs of enemy troops landing. With no sign of any enemy landings, Godbold nevertheless established a three-man outpost with a BAR to hold the bridge connecting Peale and Wake proper.

Japanese cruisers continued to provide fire support to the landing-force troops, concentrating on the airstrip and Hanna's gun, whilst Battery E's 3in. guns fired pre-arranged airbursts over the landing area. SNLF troops continued to put pressure on Maj. Putnam's defense line around Hanna's gun, which was being pressed tighter and tighter to a point where Maj. Putnam remarked to his men: "This is as far as we go." Although Putnam held his position until the surrender, he was not able to prevent enemy troops working east and joining the Kesshitai, which had landed between Peacock Point and Putnam's position, and was pushing northwards toward the underground bunkers, including Devereux's command post.

The squad from Battery D, under the command of Corp. Graves, which Devereux had sent south from his command post by truck earlier, had somehow stopped short of the point that Devereux had ordered them to by some 400yds (366m). Here they disembarked and, thinking that they were at the designated point south of the east end of the airstrip, started to work west in the darkness through the brush. Very quickly they came under enemy machine-gun and small-arms fire, which killed one Marine and pinned the rest of them down. Unable to advance farther, Graves' squad withdrew northward toward Devereux's command post where, upon arrival, they were placed in defense as part of what would become "Major Potter's line." Devereux now knew that enemy troops were in place between Peacock Point and Maj. Putnam's position, and that they were moving north toward him.

At this time, Battery E (the only remaining complete antiaircraft battery) positioned in the elbow of Wake proper, came under mortar and machine-gun fire from SNLF troops who had crossed the airstrip to the lagoon shore and were working their way east and west. Battery A also started to receive incoming mortar and light artillery fire, and as a result the battery commander, Lt. Barninger, set up a defensive perimeter with two .30-cal machine guns, using his range-section troops as infantry.

The Japanese shrine on Wake Island, dedicated not only to the Japanese killed during the battle but also to the many hundreds of Japanese troops who died of malnutrition and the frequent bombardments of Wake during the occupation. (Author's collection)

Battery E managed to silence one enemy machine gun with 3in. gunfire, but the harassing fire continued and so the battery commander, Lieutenant Lewis, formed a scratch squad of infantry (ten men) under the command of Sergeant Ramon Gragg to push west and try to lift the incoming fire on Battery E. Gragg's squad had advanced only 50yds (46m) when they were fired upon, which forced them to ground. Here they formed a defense line, taking the SNLF troops under fire and lifting the fire on Battery E. They held this line until the surrender.

At 0430hrs Devereux received word from the .50-cal machine-gun section at the east of the airstrip, commanded by Corporal McAnally, via one of Devereux's few working telephone lines that Japanese troops were attacking in force up the shore road northwards. McAnally was also still in telephone contact with the .50-cal machine-gun section dug in on the east shore 400yds (366m) south of his position. These two machine-gun sections took up coordinated fire on the advancing Japanese. Firing continued between the SNLF troops and the two machine-gun sections; McAnally maintained communication with Devereux throughout. Finally, with McAnally reporting to Devereux that his positions had been pinpointed and were coming under heavy attack, and with dawn breaking, Devereux ordered McAnally to retire to the command-post area and report to Maj. Potter.

With the defenders being hard pressed on Wake proper, and with no word from Wilkes since 0300hrs, Cdr. Cunningham sent the message to CinCPac: "Enemy on Island – issue in doubt." This message was a key factor in convincing Vice Admiral Pye that there was no point in the relief task force going any farther.

With dawn approaching, Lt. Poindexter had returned to his mobile-reserve section west of the airstrip, which was coming under increasingly accurate fire, putting one .30-cal machine gun out of action. With the increasing threat that he would be outflanked, Poindexter ordered a withdrawal by section back to Camp 1 and the remainder of the mobile reserve. Displacing by 150yd (138m) bounds, the section reached Camp 1 safely just after dawn, forming a defense line just east of the water tank.

By dawn, Maj. Putnam's men and the men of Hanna's gun were hard pressed and completely surrounded. Almost all of Putnam's men were either dead or wounded, including the gallant Captain "Hammering Hank" Elrod, who was killed throwing a grenade to break up one of the many Japanese assaults. (Elrod would receive the Medal of Honor for his bravery during the defense of Wake Island.) Also dead was the indomitable Lt. Uchida, killed leading one of the charges against Putnam's lines. Hanna, Holewinski, and the three civilian gun crewmen had taken cover under the gun platform of the 3in. gun, with only Hanna's .45 automatic and Holewinski's M1903 Springfield as weapons.

With Wake proper coming under increasing pressure from the attacking Japanese, Devereux ordered Potter to assemble as many men as he could muster and form a defense line 100yds (91m) south of the command post. At the same time Devereux telephoned Capt. Godbold on Peale, ordering him to send all Battery D troops, including the .50-cal machine-gun sections (30 officers and men) by truck to the command post and report to Major Potter.

Daybreak found Lt. Kliewer and his three Marines still at their post, despite attacks throughout the night. With the dawn came a concerted effort by the Japanese to eliminate the Marines with a bayonet charge, but with the aid of one of the .50-cal machine-gun sections at the west end of the airstrip, Kliewer was again able to hold his position.

At Camp 1, Lt. Poindexter had, by daybreak, tied in his defense line, which now totaled 40 riflemen with ten .30-cal machine guns. On Peale, with the departure of Capt. Godbold and his Battery D troops, only Battery B remained under the command of Lt. Kessler. As day broke Kessler scanned Wilkes across the lagoon, to be greeted by the sight of numerous Japanese flags flying. This he reported to Maj. Devereux, who could conclude only that Wilkes had fallen. Kessler also observed the "superstructure of a grounded destroyer," this being *Patrol Boat 33* on Wake's southern shore, and, receiving permission from Maj. Devereux, opened fire, his first salvo shooting away the mainmast. Subsequent hits on the superstructure and upper hull caused the ship to catch fire. At 0645hrs the three ships of Destroyer Division 30, led by the destroyer *Mutsuki*, came within range off Battery B on Peale, which opened fire, scoring hits on the *Mutsuki* before all three ships retired out of range.

With dawn now fully up, the *Soryu* and *Hiryu* launched every plane in a maximum air effort against Wake in support of the SNLF troops, continuously swooping down from 6,000ft (1,830m) at any US installation or position they could identify, with only Battery E's guns and .50-cal machine guns to oppose them.

By 0700hrs the position on Wake looked very bad to Maj. Devereux. With no word from Wilkes or Poindexter's men, Japanese aircraft attacking at will, enemy troops advancing on his command post and the sight of so many enemy ships out to sea, presumably carrying more landing-force troops, Devereux conferred with Cdr. Cunningham, asking whether any friendly forces were at hand to relieve them. Cunningham replied that there were no friendly forces within 24 hours of Wake, and as such, at 0700hrs, Cunningham ordered the island surrendered to the Japanese.

Japanese troops come ashore in the film *Wake Island*, released in 1942. In reality these men would of course would be much more widely dispersed. They also landed in darkness, as opposed to daylight as portrayed in the film. (Getty)

Maj. Devereux asked Cunningham if he could try and contact the Japanese by radio, to which Cunningham agreed. On hanging up the telephone, Marine Gunner Hamas entered Devereux's bunker to give the major an update on the situation outside. Finishing his report, Hamas asked if he had any further orders for Maj. Potter on the defense line. Devereux answered: "It's too late John, Cdr. Cunningham has ordered us to surrender. Fix up a white flag and pass the word to cease fire." Hamas stared at Devereux in disbelief, but after a few seconds answered "Yes, Sir." As Hamas walked from the command post he shouted: "Major's orders, we're surrendering, major's orders." Devereux rushed to the door and screamed after Hamas: "It's not my orders, God damn it!" At that, Devereux, with Sergeant Malleck carrying a white flag, went down the access road south from his command post to locate the Japanese.

Meanwhile, on Wilkes, at 0245hrs the .50-cal machine guns had opened fire on Japanese landing craft heard offshore in the darkness. In the light from the searchlights that the strongpoint commander, Captain Platt, had ordered

TOP
Japanese bunker on Wake's southern shore, December 2009, built by CPNAB forced labor in 1942. (Author's collection)

BOTTOM
Airplane revetments on the old airfield, December 2009, built by CPNAB forced labor after the fall of Wake. (Author's collection)

Situation on Wake Island at time of surrender

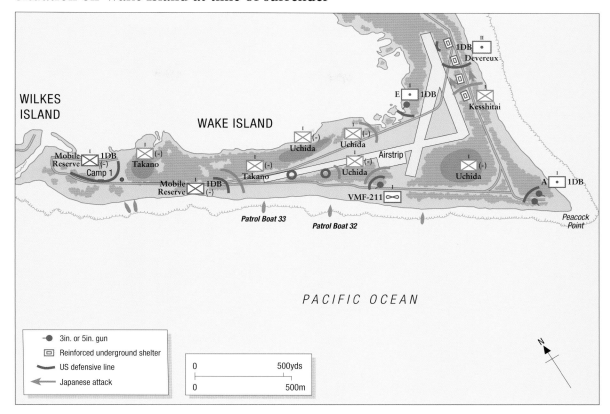

switched on (although the searchlight died a few minutes later because of the damage caused in the previous dynamite explosion), the "100 picked men" of the Takano Unit in two landing craft were observed landing virtually under the muzzles of Battery F's two remaining 3in. guns. Takano's men also came under fire from the two .50-cal machine guns located on the shore to the west.

Captain Platt ordered Battery L (5in.) to send two gun sections to the lagoon shore and take up positions at the new channel toward Kuku Point. At the same time, Battery L's fire-control men, along with headquarters personnel led by Lt. McAlister, took up prepared positions on the seaward beach between the new channel and Battery F (3in.). McAlister established his command post at the nearby searchlight section.

Prior to losing contact, Maj. Devereux had warned Platt to reinforce his two .30-cal machine-gun sections located north of Kuku Point to cover any attempted landings on the lagoon shore on Wilkes.

Previously, Battery F, commanded by Gunner McKinstry with his makeshift gun crew of Marine searchlight operators, sailors, and civilians, had orders from Capt. Platt in the event of an enemy landing to fire antiboat missions until his 3in. guns could be depressed no further and then to protect McAlister's section.

As the searchlight flickered out, McKinstry opened fire on the barges with 3in. shells cut for muzzle burst. At the same time, McAlister sent out a two-man grenadier party to pelt the landing craft. Accurate return fire from the Japanese troops killed one and wounded the other, who managed to return to McAlister's lines.

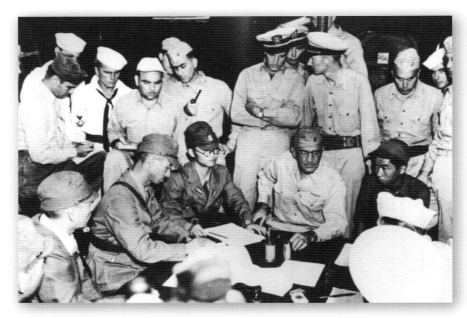

Signing of the formal surrender of Wake Island, September 4, 1945, on board the USS *Levy*. It was signed by Rear Admiral Sakaibara Shigematsu, Garrison Commander. Seated, accepting the surrender, is Brigadier General Sanderson. Standing to his left with pipe in hand is Colonel Walter Bayler, "the last man off Wake" in December 1941. (USMC)

Takano's troops pushed inland from the beach toward McKinstry's gun position and also to the west toward Battery L at Kuku Point. As the SNLF troops closed in on Battery F's position, fierce hand-to-hand fighting ensued, but McKinstry, realizing he was outnumbered by a factor of ten to one, and that his position could not be held much longer, after stripping the firing blocks off the 3in. guns, directed a withdrawal east to McAlister's position. The Japanese initially pursued McKinstry's withdrawal, but accurate rifle fire halted them, who retired to the now-vacated Battery F gun position.

To the west the only thing in the way of the Japanese advance was a lone .50-cal machine gun on the beach. This lone gun with its two-man crew kept Takano's men pinned down and managed to repel all attempts to silence it all throughout the night.

By 0400hrs the situation on Wilkes was somewhat stabilized, but, having lost most of his wire communications, Capt. Platt realized he could not control the action from his command post and so moved his it to machine-gun post number 11 on the seaward shoreline. From his new command post Platt set out in the darkness to reconnoiter the situation himself. Upon his return, having observed that most of the enemy troops were massed around the abandoned Battery F position, Capt. Platt ordered Platoon Sergeant Coulson to collect the two .30-cal machine guns from Kuku Point, plus the searchlight crew and anyone else he came across, and join him at machine-gun position number 10 on the beach. Sergeant Coulson returned within 25 minutes with his two machine guns, plus their crews and eight riflemen. Platt briefed his makeshift squad; they would move forward as close to Battery F's position as they could without being detected and then, with the two .30-cal machine guns giving flanking fire, assault the Japanese position. Orders to the machine-gunners were to fire short bursts, well aimed and low, to prevent firing on McAlister and McKinstry's men. By painstaking maneuvering in the early dawn, Platt and his men managed to get within 50yds (46m) of the enemy pocket, and on order from Platt the two machine guns opened fire and Platt with his eight-man skirmish line swept forward against the 70 SNLF troops.

At almost the same time, on the other side of the Japanese pocket, Lt. McAlister observed a six-man Japanese patrol working east along the beach. McAlister's men opened fire on the patrol, killing one, with the rest taking cover behind a huge coral head on the beach. Gunner McKinstry's Marines fanned out around both flanks of the Japanese position and, keeping them under fire, Gunner McKinstry and PFC William Halstead climbed on top of the rock and dispatched the remaining five SNLF troops.

After taking care of the Japanese patrol, Gunner McKinstry joined forces with Lt. McAlister and attacked the Japanese pocket at Battery F at the same time as Capt. Platt was assaulting it from the west. The Japanese, faced with attacks from east and west, panicked, taking cover wherever they could. One group of 30 SNLF troops took cover under and around the abandoned Marine searchlight truck, and were fired upon by one of Platt's .30-cal machine guns, killing them all.

Immediately after their successful assault, Capt. Platt assigned Lt. McAlister to form a ten-man squad to mop up the position whilst he took a similar squad to sweep the island. With the exception of two wounded SNLF troops, no other live Japanese troops were encountered, and it would seem that the Takano "chosen men" had been wiped out to a man. As part of his mopping-up operations McAlister had all the Japanese flags that had been placed around the gun position removed, but unfortunately they had already been reported to Maj. Devereux by Lt. Kessler on Peale.

At 0700hrs, whilst Capt. Platt was reorganizing his forces, Japanese aircraft dived on Kuku Point's 5in. battery. These attacks continued throughout the morning, with only .50-cal machine guns able to fire back. At 0800hrs Capt. Platt again tried to raise Maj. Devereux's command post but succeeded only in contacting Lt. Poindexter at Camp 1, who was also not in contact with Maj. Devereux. Neither of them knew that by this time the island had already been surrendered.

Throughout the morning Capt. Platt reorganized his positions on Wilkes, and around noon received word that enemy landing boats were sighted heading for Wake proper, these transports along with several other warships having closed to within 4,000yds (3,660m) of the island, well within the range of Battery L's 5in. guns on Kuku Point. Platt immediately ordered Lt. McAlister to man his guns, but upon reaching the guns McAlister found Gun 1's training mechanism inoperative, so that it could not track a target, and Gun 2's recoil cylinder had been riddled by bomb fragments, so neither gun was operational. Platt inspected the guns personally, then returned to the two 3in. guns at Battery F, but they too would not fire again.

In desperation, Capt. Platt ordered Lt. McAlister and Gunner McKinstry to assemble all possible men along with the two .30-cal machine guns and head down to the old channel and engage the enemy as soon as possible. Platt joined the rest of his command, but they came under fire from a Japanese destroyer, which, seeing that Wilkes' guns were out of commission, had moved in to a distance of 2,000yds (1,830m) offshore and commenced shelling the island. Inexplicably, the destroyer ceased firing around 1300hrs, and as Platt and his men headed east in a skirmish line toward Wake proper around 1330hrs they observed three men, two wearing khaki, one of whom was carrying a white flag, and a third man wearing green who was carrying a large sword. Moving forward, Capt. Platt was confronted by Maj. Devereux, who informed him that the island had surrendered. Platt just looked at him in disbelief.

AFTERMATH

As Maj. Devereux moved out from his command post, he passed the word to surrender to all units still in telephone contact, these being Batteries A and E on Wake proper, Battery B on Peale, and the few .50-cal machine-gun positions that still had their telephone wires intact.

All units were ordered to destroy all weapons and matériel as best they could, leaving as little as possible for the Japanese. At Battery A, after destroying what they could, Lt. Barninger ordered his men to eat as much as possible (a wise move as it turned out, since they would get nothing to eat for the next two days). As Devereux passed through "Potter's line" he ordered all men to cease firing and lay down their weapons. The Marines obeyed Devereux's order, some stripping the bolt from their rifles and throwing it into the brush.

The Stars and Stripes flies once again over Wake Island following the atoll's surrender in 1945. (USMC)

Devereux and Sgt. Malleck headed south toward the Marine aid station, from which they had heard no word for some time. It had in fact already been captured by the Japanese. Halfway to the aid station they were confronted by a lone Japanese soldier, who motioned for them to remove their pistol belts and helmets, before ushering them toward the aid station. On arrival, Devereux found that everyone at the aid station, wounded and hospital personnel alike, had been removed from the bunker and tied up with telephone wire around their hands behind their backs; they also had nooses around their necks.

Devereux met with an officer who spoke some English and explained as best he could that the island had surrendered. Shortly afterwards, Cdr. Cunningham arrived at the aid station in his pickup truck. After giving the order to surrender, Cunningham had returned to his bungalow at Camp 2, washed, shaved and changed into his blue uniform before returning.

Devereux left Cdr. Cunningham with the Japanese officer to sort out details of the surrender whilst he and Sgt. Malleck, accompanied by another Japanese officer (who, when asked by Devereux if he spoke English, replied in perfect English, "No, do you speak Japanese?"), made their way across Wake proper and onto Wilkes to locate any survivors and give them word of the surrender.

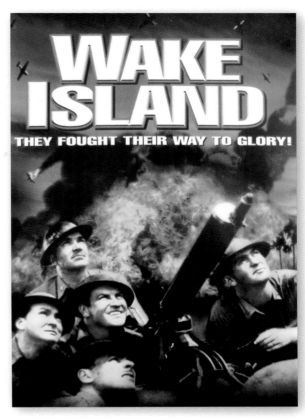

Hollywood's version of the battle of Wake Island. Said to have been produced from official Marine Corps records, it contained numerous errors, including the island's Navy commander being killed on the first day and there subsequently being an all-Marine Corps defense, culminating in the deaths of all the defenders. This gave a totally inaccurate impression of the battle for Wake Island, but did inspire hundreds of thousands of Americans to volunteer to swell the USMC to avenge the men who fought on Wake Island. (USMC)

Upon reaching Maj. Putnam's position around Hanna's gun, they found the whole area strewn with dead and wounded, both Marine and Japanese. Of the men of VMF-211 only ten had survived, nine of whom were wounded, including Maj. Putnam. Captain Tharin was the only unwounded officer. Lieutenant Hanna, Corp. Holewinski, and one of the three civilian volunteers were wounded; the other two civilians were dead.

Lieutenant Kliewer and his three-man detail were still trying to start the generator needed to blow up the airstrip, when Devereux reached them, calling out to them that the island had surrendered. One of Kliewer's Marines cried: "Don't surrender lieutenant, Marines never surrender!"

At around 1115hrs the surrender party reached the Japanese lines facing Lt. Poindexter's counterattack. Devereux passed through the Japanese lines under fire from the Marines, came upon Lt. Poindexter, and informed him of the surrender. "Aw shucks" was Poindexter's only answer.

Upon reaching Camp 1, still held by Poindexter's mobile reserve, one of the accompanying Japanese soldiers, on seeing the Stars and Stripes still flying from the water tower, climbed up and cut the colors down for a souvenir.

Maj. Devereux and the surrender party next crossed over to Wilkes. At first there was no sign of life, but eventually Devereux was confronted by, as he put it "a few grubby, dirty men who came out of the brush with their rifles ready." Captain Platt was given the word and all his men laid down their arms and awaited the Japanese.

Throughout December 23 the Japanese rounded up the survivors. Stripped and bound, they were herded onto the airstrip where they were made to kneel, facing machine guns; their worst fears about Japanese treatment of prisoners appeared to be about to come true. The SNLF troops were raging over the number of their dead all over Wake and Wilkes and they wanted vengeance for their fallen comrades. Only with the timely appearance of a high-ranking naval officer, Rear Admiral Kajioka, resplendent in dress-white uniform, and after much heated discussion, were the machine guns stood down.

All the men on Wake were treated as prisoners of war, including the civilians. They were moved from the airstrip and held in several of the surviving barrack huts at Camp 2; the officers and Dan Teters were held in two of the surviving bungalows. All the prisoners were used as forced labor to clean up Wake.

In January 1942 the *Nitta Maru* arrived off Wake to take the prisoners to prison camps in China. Some 388 civilian contractors and the wounded were retained on Wake to construct the Japanese defenses and airstrip. Of the men kept on Wake as laborers, 45 died of malnutrition. About 200 were shipped to Japan in September 1942, leaving 98 specialist contractors on Wake. These were all machine-gunned to death (except one who escaped and was later found hiding and beheaded) in October 1943. Admiral Sakibura, the island commander, was tried and hanged for this war crime in 1947.

The men shipped in to China in January 1942 on the *Nitta Maru* endured two weeks of hell, with starvation rations and daily beatings. Five men, Seamen 2nd Class Franklin Theodore, John W. Lambert, and Roy H. Gonzales from Patrol Wing 2 USN, along with Master Technical Sergeant Earl R. Hannum and Technical Sergeant Vincent W. Bailey, both from VMF-211, were taken on deck and, after charges were read to them in Japanese, were made to kneel and were beheaded, their headless bodies then being mutilated before being thrown overboard. No Japanese were ever brought to trial for these murders, but an inquiry conducted by Gunner Hamas in October 1946 identified Lt. Toshio Saito IJN, who commanded the guard on the *Nitta Maru*, as the one who gave the order to execute the men.

Colonel Walter Bayler, the last Marine off Wake in December 1941, was the first to set foot back on the atoll in September 1945. (USMC)

THE CUNNINGHAM–DEVEREUX CONTROVERSY

Back in America, "Wake's Marines" had given the American people hope that although the going would be tough, final victory would be theirs and Wake Island along with Pearl Harbor would be avenged. But, with the press and even Hollywood, with their forthcoming movie *Wake Island*, making the battle for Wake an all-Marine Corps event, much controversy would emerge after the war with the return of the men from Wake, in particular over the roles of Major Devereux and Commander Cunningham. President Roosevelt did not help the situation at all when he addressed the nation on the fall of Wake:

THE WHITE HOUSE
WASHINGTON

5 January 1942

Citation by

THE PRESIDENT OF THE UNITED STATES

of

The Wake detachment of the 1st Defense Battalion, U. S.
Marine Corps, under command of Major James P. S. Devereux,
U. S. Marines

and

Marine Fighting Squadron 211 of Marine Aircraft Group 21,
under command of Major Paul A. Putnam, U. S. Marines

"The courageous conduct of the officers and men
of these units, who defended Wake Island against an
overwhelming superiority of enemy air, sea, and land
attack from December 8 to 22, 1941, has been noted
with admiration by their fellow countrymen and the
civilized world, and will not be forgotten so long
as gallantry and heroism are respected and honored.
These units are commended for their devotion to duty
and splendid conduct at their battle stations under
most adverse conditions. With limited defensive
means against attacks in great force, they manned
their shore installations and flew their aircraft
so well that five enemy warships were either sunk
or severely damaged, many hostile planes shot down,
and an unknown number of land troops destroyed."

Franklin D Roosevelt

LEFT
Major Devereux hugs his son in 1945 after returning to the US after the Japanese surrender. He had spent the last four years as a POW, after being captured by the Japanese after the fall of Wake Island. (Getty)

RIGHT
The Presidential Unit Citation issued by President Franklin D. Roosevelt on January 5, 1942. This particular one was issued direct from the White House and was for the 1st Defense Battalion USMC and VMF-211 only. This further fueled the conception that the defense of Wake Island was purely a US Marine Corps "show," and aggravated the controversy between Cunningham and Devereux.
(USMC)

BELOW LEFT
Standard small arms used by the SNLF. (Top) 7.7mm Nambu Type 99 light machine gun; Type 97 hand grenade. (Rifles, top to bottom) "Last-ditch" 6.5mm weapon produced in February 1945; 7.7mm Type 99 Arisaka long rifle; short Type 99.

BELOW RIGHT
When a Japanese soldier was sent into combat it was customary for his family, neighbors, and comrades to sign a national flag for him with wishes of good fortune.

There were only some four hundred United States Marines who, in the heroic and historic defense of Wake Island, inflicted such great losses on the enemy. Some of these men were killed in action and others are now prisoners of war. When the survivors of that great fight are liberated and restored to their homes they will learn that a hundred and thirty million of their fellow citizens have been inspired to render their own full share of service and sacrifice.

Roosevelt also commended only the Wake detachment of the 1st Defense Battalion and VMF-211 in his Presidential Unit Citation of January 5, 1942. Commander Cunningham would eventually be awarded this citation many years later, along with the other Navy and Army personnel who fought on Wake.

The controversy of who was in command of Wake Island during the 16-day siege, Cdr. Cunningham or Maj. Devereux, originated from the US Navy's press releases.

From the first day's bombing on December 8, Cdr. Cunningham had sent daily status reports from Wake to Naval Headquarters, Pearl Harbor. The Navy issued no press releases on the situation at Wake until the defenders successfully repelled the first Japanese invasion attempt on December 11.

On the afternoon of December 11 the Navy disclosed that Wake's "Marine garrison" had repelled "light naval units," sinking at least two naval vessels, but made no reference to either Cunningham or Devereux as being in command. From then on the American press released daily updates on Wake's "small band of Devil Dogs."

On December 24 the Navy Department announced the fall of Wake, but once again mentioned only that the garrison of 13 Marine officers, 365 enlisted Marines, one Navy medial officer, and six Navy corpsmen were either dead or captured, again with no mention of the garrison's Navy commanding officer. Instead, they identified Maj. Devereux as being in command. It is thought that the Navy did not wish to be identified with any more bad news after Pearl Harbor.

On January 18, 1942, monitored Japanese radio broadcasts announced the arrival of 1,235 prisoners of war from Wake Island, including the island's commander, Cdr. Cunningham.

Quizzed by the press, the Navy finally recognized that Cdr. Cunningham had been on Wake as "Officer in Charge of Naval Operations," again with no mention of his being in overall command.

Throughout the war years the Wake Island Marines' and Maj. Devereux's fame grew and all thoughts of Cdr. Cunningham fell by the wayside. Upon returning to the United States at the war's end, Maj. Devereux returned to ticker-tape parades as the "hero of Wake," whilst Cdr. Cunningham returned to the Navy in obscurity. Expecting to be possibly court-martialed for surrendering Wake to the Japanese, Cunningham was treated with indifference even to the point where the Navy claimed that they had no record of his even being on Wake Island at all.

US Marine Corps monument to the 1st Defense Battalion and VMF-211, located on the lagoon side of the airport building alongside Maj. Devereux's command bunker. (Author's collection)

A group of SNLF troops of the 2nd Shanghai unit pose aboard the IJN destroyer *Hiyodori* in June 1937.

In February and March 1946 Maj. Devereux published a four-part article on the siege of Wake Island in the *Saturday Evening Post* entitled "This is how it was." This was followed by a book, *The Story of Wake Island*. In both he made little mention of Cdr. Cunningham, which infuriated the former island commander.

In 1947 the Marine Corps published their official account of "The Defense of Wake" by Colonel Heinl. Received as being the definitive account of the battle, Col. Heinl not surprisingly played down the involvement of the Navy and the Army at Wake, concentrating on the involvement of the 1st Defense Battalion and VMF-211 under the command of Majors Devereux and Putnam.

Cunningham continued to lobby anyone who would listen to have him recognized for what he did on Wake, even enlisting the help of former Marine officers stationed on Wake during the siege, but as time passed by Wake disappeared into the annals of history, even Cunningham's book, *Wake Island Command*, released in 1961, did little to help the former island commander.

The Devereux–Cunningham controversy will probably never go away, but the whole garrison, be they Navy, Army, Marine or civilian, will always be remembered with these words, written by Major Putnam on December 21, 1941: "All hands have behaved splendidly and held up in a manner of which the Marine Corps may well tell."

THE BATTLEFIELD TODAY

The Japanese garrison under the command of Admiral Sakibara surrendered on September 4, 1945. The first Marine to step onto Wake was Colonel Walter Bayler who, in December 1941, had been the "last man off Wake."

After World War II Wake remained under the jurisdiction of the US Navy. PanAm resumed their clipper service to China and the Philippines, but this was short-lived after the advent of long-range commercial airlines.

After World War II Wake was used as a military staging post during the Korean and Vietnam wars. It was the location of the meeting between President Truman and General Douglas McArthur during the Korean War, which resulted in McArthur being relieved of his command.

Recently, Wake has suffered several typhoons that have almost leveled the atoll. Access is still restricted, even though Wake no longer has any military personnel stationed there and is used only for emergency landings. In 2009, Valor Tours, in cooperation with Military Historical Tours, secured permission to land on Wake with veterans and historians of the battle (including this author). Still to be seen on the island are relics of the battle,

A photograph of the "98 Rock," taken in December 2009. The words: "98 US PW 5-10-43" were inscribed by an unknown POW on Wake, recording the 98 remaining prisoners of war who were subsequently executed in October 1943. (Author's collection)

including two 3in. antiaircraft guns, one at the airport building and the other in the area of Camp 2. Memorials to the US Marine Corps, US Navy, and CPNAB contractors, as well as a monument to the Japanese are to be found to the east of the airstrip alongside the igloo bunkers, three of which remain: Maj. Devereux's command post, Cdr. Cunningham's command post, and the Marine hospital. Many of the Japanese fortifications built by the CPNAB prisoners also remain.

On Wilkes is the "98 rock," a coral boulder inscribed by an unknown prisoner with: "98 US PW 5-10-43," a memorial to the 98 prisoners of war machine-gunned by the Japanese.

The bridge across from Wake proper to Peale Island was destroyed in the last typhoon and has not been rebuilt, so access to the remains of the PanAm Village is difficult. Wilkes has been declared a bird sanctuary, and access is allowed only as far as the "98 rock." The rest of Wilkes is overgrown.

A small museum in the airport building contains many artifacts that have been uncovered over the years, including parts of aircraft (both US and Japanese), personal items, and several machine guns.

Troops of the 1st Maizuru SNLF posing for a photograph in Hainan, China, in 1939. All are carrying the 7.7mm Type 99 rifle, except for the sailor at front right, who has a 6.5mm Type 38 rifle. (Eric Doody)

BIBLIOGRAPHY

After-action reports by 1st Defense Battalion personnel

Bayler, Walter L. J. and Carnes, Cecil, "Last Man Off Wake Island" in the *Saturday Evening Post* of April 17, 1943, Bobbs-Merrill: Indianapolis, 1943

Cohen, Stan, *Enemy on Island, Issue in Doubt*, Pictorial Histories Publishing Company: Missoula, MT, 1983Cressman, Robert J., *A Magnificent Fight: the battle for Wake Island*, Naval Institute Press, 1995

Cunningham, W. Scott and Sims, Lydel, *Wake Island Command*, New York Popular Library: New York, 1962

Devereux, James, *The Story of Wake Island*, J. B. Lippincott: Philadelphia, 1947

Dull, Paul, *A Battle History of the Imperial Japanese Navy (1941–1945)*, Naval Institute Press: Annapolis, 1978

Gandt, Robert, *China Clipper, the Age of the Great Seaplanes*, Naval Institute Press: Annapolis, 1991

Heinl Jr., Robert Debs, *The Defense of Wake*, History and Museums Division, HQ US Marine Corps: Washington, DC, 1947

Kessler, Woodrow M., *To Wake and beyond: Reminiscences,* HQ US Marine Corps History and Museums Division: Washington, DC, 1988

Kinney, John F. and McCaffrey, James M., *Wake Island Pilot: a World War II Memoir*, Brassey's: Washington, DC, 1995

Poindexter, Arthur A., "Our last Hurrah on Wake" in *American History Illustrated*, February 1992

"Wake Island; America's First Victory" in *Leatherneck* magazine, December 1991

Moran, Jim, *US Marine Corps Uniforms & Equipment in World War II*, Windrow & Greene: London, 1992

Updegraph Jr., Charles L., *US Marine Corps Special Units of World War II*, History and Museums Division, HQ US Marine Corps: Washington, DC, 1979

Urwin, Gregory J. W., *Facing Fearful Odds*, University of Nebraska Press, 1997

INDEX

References to illustrations are shown in **bold**.